REMARKABLE YOU

Build a Personal Brand and Take Charge of Your Career

CHRIS DESSI

REMARKABLE YOU

Build a Personal Brand and
Take Charge of Your Career

ISBN 978-1-61961-373-7

LIONCREST
PUBLISHING

In memory of my Father, Adrian Dessi.
You were a remarkable man.

CONTENTS

For all the tools mentioned in this book, go to
ChristopherDessi.com/resources

FOREWORD

IN REMARKABLE YOU, CHRIS DESSI PUSHES YOU TO build your personal brand, and take charge of your career. In the C-Suite, Brand is a promise delivered. What is the promise that you deliver to the world? You have to stand for something. You have to tell the world what makes you remarkable. What value do you bring to God's good earth?

Just like Chris Dessi is not your average executive, Remarkable You is not an average book. What began with me working with Chris to keynote his event has evolved into a friendship anchored in mutual admiration. I've seen Chris in action, and I'm impressed. I was a C-Suite officer at a fortune 100. I worked shoulder to shoulder with the most talented, relentless and dynamic executives in the world. They are an elite group. Chris Dessi is an elite executive.

See, I look for problem solvers, not problem seekers. Chris is a problem solver. We're kindred spirits in that regard. I bring the C-Suite to those who want to learn. I bring them together at my events, radio shows, television shows and books. He brings people together through his agency, speaking engagements, online courses, events, books, and television appearances.

Chris is a risk taker too. The pillars he shares in Remarkable You are his personal secrets he's leveraged to become a huge success. Risk is paralyzing for many. Chris took the risks for you, so you don't have to. Real leaders and people who are relentless deliver on promises. Chris makes big promises in this book. He delivers for you.

What is it that you want? What is it that you want to drive? You have to paint a vision, and sell a story. But you have to make it better. Make your story better. Make the value you bring bigger. You're taking a huge first step in the right direction with Remarkable You.

I encourage you to follow Chris' guidance in this compelling book. Be the biggest baddest version of yourself. Be Remarkable.

> — JEFFREY HAYZLETT, PRIMETIME TV & RADIO
> HOST, KEYNOTE SPEAKER, BEST-SELLING
> AUTHOR AND GLOBAL BUSINESS CELEBRITY

PREFACE: THE $260,000 BLOG POST

THIS BOOK IS ABOUT CHALLENGING YOURSELF TO have more, be more, and do more. Events in my life led me to do a series of things that I want you to do: feel insecure; get a little bit angry and focused; stop seeking permission; and, finally, use the tools of social media to execute your decision. Do these things and you can control your fate.

I wanted to be a vice president of marketing but knew I couldn't get there in my current position. Instead, I wrote a blog post about what I would do in that capacity. When I interviewed for a job with a new company a month later, they really wanted to know more about the ideas I had discussed in the blog. I got the job. I didn't sit back and wait for someone to tell me I could be a vice president. I decided to make it happen.

The phenomenon of social media allows you to create the tools necessary to achieve those lofty goals, but they won't do you any good if you do not have the hunger and the commitment to have more and be more. If you do have that drive, I'll show you how to use those tools to extraordinary effect.

And while it's not my intention to scare you, the truth is that we're at the kindergarten stage of social media technology and at the rate the technology is compounding, we're going to be at the PhD stage in a year and half, and if you don't keep up, you'll be left behind.

My five-year-old can navigate iPhones and iPads, and there's nothing foreign about it. On the contrary, it's native to the manner in which children learn, built in and intrinsically baked into their education. By virtue of that, by the time they join the workforce, they will most likely have launched, executed, and managed their own businesses, will be much more self-reliant as entrepreneurs, and be not at all reliant on big business and corporate America for their livelihoods.

As I write this, 300 executives have just been laid off at the ESPN sports network. These people who had thought that their jobs had been secure were let go because of a shift in the way that people—particularly young people—are consuming media. The fact is, they are moving away from cable TV, preferring to get their content on their computers and mobile devices. In fact, the network is scrambling to figure out new ways to deliver and monetize their content to a generation that has no particular ties to the ESPN brand. If the company doesn't reposition fast enough, another network will come along and completely replace it.

As for the executives who now find themselves out of a job, many will have to begin the job hunt anew, putting together their résumés, contacting colleagues about work, checking the employment sites, and so on. If you've ever been let go, you know the drill. Others, however, had already begun the process long before the pink slip arrived. How did they know? Had they seen the handwriting on the wall? Maybe, but not necessarily. They were simply prepared for the eventuality because they were proactively creating and maintaining their own individual brands.

When news of the mass layoffs broke, I wrote a blog outlining the five things those executives should be doing, which includes: improving their LinkedIn profiles; launching their own personal blogs using their first and last names; leveraging their network of people; targeting the companies they want to work for with, perhaps, a website like Xcompanyshouldhireme.com; and taking informational interviews.

Let me explain how just that very last point would make a difference in this real-world instance. If you've been taking informational interviews, you already have context with those people. They now have skin in the game on your behalf. You've approached them without wanting anything from them. Maybe you gleaned some information from them and maybe you provided them with some.

Suppose you had asked the people in your network something like, "If money were no object and you were able to create a company tomorrow that would magically solve your biggest problem that you encountered today, what would that company do?" The answer to that question might be the beginning of your next entrepreneurial venture.

In the case at hand, maybe you had explained what you did at ESPN. Now when the names are released—these are executives, after all, not entry-level employees—your network of people might wonder if you were one of the unlucky ones, and so they'll turn to Google to find out.

Now, if you've been actively engaging in blogging under your name, when they look you up they will discover that you haven't just been fortified within your little compound, waiting for retirement. On the contrary, they'll see that you've been engaging with others in different companies and maybe different fields. Perhaps you've talked about companies that you admire, other executives you respect, or ideas you have that demonstrate your acuity. So now, you're not just a clock-puncher—you're a thought leader concerned with the larger world. And that's very attractive to your next employer.

If you are one of these executives and you had been following the tenants I set forth in *Remarkable You*, you would have already created or joined a LinkedIn group of like-minded individuals that will now serve as your support base. While others are panicked, sending desperate messages to headhunters saying, "I've got to update my résumé! Oh my god, I have a wife and two kids and a mortgage," you, having followed my advice, would simply post to the group, saying something like:

"I'm on to the next chapter of my life. If anybody would like to meet with me for coffee tomorrow morning, I'll be at the Starbucks on Main from 10:00 to 11:30 a.m. I'm taking all ideas and listening to everybody, and, oh, by the way, I've generated these blog posts—here's some food for thought for the conversation tomorrow if you're around."

You will have already installed the SumoMe app and begun aggregating your contacts' emails. So here are, say, 20 to 50 emails of people interested in the content you've been developing, whom you can simply email to explain that you are on the next step of your journey.

Imagine that while producing sports programming, you discover that your real passion is horses. You figure out late in life that what you truly desire is to have a 50-acre horse farm in Maine. Well, you've just been laid off. How do you suddenly transition into that ideal life? Chances are, you don't. You take what you can get so that you can pay your bills.

If, on the other hand, you've been blogging about raising horses in Maine and you send out an email to your group saying that you've finally left ESPN and are headed to Maine to raise horses, well, you've already got an interested group of readers who have been following and probably sharing your content and commenting on it. These are people—by virtue of their intently engaging with you on the topic—who likely have connections to the Maine horse-raising community, and since they're in your network, should be helpful in assisting you.

The bottom line is that whether you feel secure within your job or not, your job might go away. The company might go away. Your whole industry might literally go away because of a technological shift that's occurring, and by building your professional brand, you are taking the first step in the right direction for creating a safety net. Insulating your personal brand is a full-on safety net that covers your entire world, whether that be in your job, your personal life, your social life, or your hobbies.

At the very least, you've taken that first step to be a part of and have some elementary level of understanding to be able to engage with the community, speak the lingo, and not sound like a complete outsider. It may have been cute two, three, four years ago to say "I am a technological dummy," but it's not cute anymore. Frankly, it's irresponsible.

The reality now is that you will come off sounding like someone explaining the care and maintenance of your horse-and-buggy while everyone else is discussing the inner workings of a V8 Ford Mustang engine. Either you've moved into the future or you're stuck in the past. No matter how well you tend to your horse, how educated you are about feeding it or disposing of its dung off the street, no matter how well you maintain your buggy, this is the age of the automobile, and you are an anachronism.

Getting laid off can be the worst day of your life (and more on that later) or it can be the best thing that has ever happened to your career. If you've gone out on five informational interviews, maybe you have five new business ideas. Three of those might be too pie-in-the-sky. Two are decent. One of those actually has legs. You create a 10 page PowerPoint presentation with a 4 page business plan, which you put into the hands of your network. Congratulations, your career 2.0, as an entrepreneur, has just begun.

In this book, I will explain how you can take control of your destiny and insulate yourself against the whims of a fickle corporate world that sends jobs abroad, automates them, or, in the case mentioned above, simply dissolves them in an attempt to adapt to a changing world. I've been through it and I emerged more secure—personally as well as financially— than ever before. And so can you.

FROM DIAL-UP TO BLOW-UP

"I firmly believe that luck is the residue of design; it does not happen unless you put yourself in position to succeed."
— RAYMOND SANSEVERINO, PARTNER AND CHAIR, REAL ESTATE DEPARTMENT, LOEB & LOEB LLP

MY LIFE TOOK A FATEFUL TURN DURING MY JUNIOR year at Loyola University when I was accepted into the Erasmus Program at Catholic University in Leuven, Belgium. The program included students from around the globe and I found myself surrounded by new ideas. As a psychology major, I was taking an industrial and organizational psychology course. I had been terrified of business courses under the assumption that they included mathematics. I was stronger in the humanities—history, English, literature.

But there in Leuven, I was shoulder to shoulder with students working on their Executive MBA degrees. We studied things like the layout and format of a retail operation and the psychology of moving people through a retail destination, and the reason why casinos don't have clocks or windows, and why the hotel rooms are so ugly (to keep you out and gambling).

I was fascinated by the intriguing course. I began scratching my head, though, realizing that some of these other students, getting Executive MBA credit for their business courses, were getting B's while I was getting A's. Meanwhile, my credits were being applied to an undergraduate psychology degree.

When I returned to the US, I talked to my father, a direct marketer all his life and my mentor in business. I told him, "I think I'm pretty good at this business thing and that there's more to it than I thought, but I think I can find a path here. I'm going to change my major."

My parents were both happy that I'd made the self-discovery but told me they didn't have the money to keep me at Loyola for an extra year. "Wrap up your undergraduate degree in psychology and we'll see how that goes," they said.

I graduated in 1997 while everyone was off becoming dot-com millionaires. I knew I wanted to be one, too. But my father, who described the Internet as "direct marketing on steroids," explained that no one in the industry was going to hire a young man with a degree in psychology.

"You need some marketing and business chops," he said. He recommended that I investigate a brand new program at New York University, where he had a friend sitting on the advisory board.

I enrolled in a Master's degree program at NYU's School of Continued Professional Studies and worked like a beast, afraid of embarrassing my father, who had gotten me into the program. I graduated with straight A's. I had found something that I was passionate about.

As I look back, my sudden interest in business while in Belgium and my father's help in getting me into the graduate program at NYU were the two defining moments that changed the trajectory of my career.

After graduation, I was able to infuse the concepts I had learned in psychology into a business environment. I interned everywhere that would have me because neither I nor my father knew whether I would be stronger on the client side or the agency side. I interned at investment banks and agencies, but eventually decided I belonged on the client side.

My first job was with Time Warner Book of the Month Club doing direct marketing. It was a very slow-moving corporation and late to adopt the dot-com movement. That, of course, caused me a lot of frustration. So, in February of 2000, with my degree in my back pocket, I jumped ship. I was 24 and ready to take over the world.

I landed at a company called Mediaplex and the sizzle started.

It was here where I fell in love with the Internet and everything it represented.

There were about 15 of us in the New York office. On Wednesday of my first week, we were all flown out to headquarters in San Francisco for the IPO party and to meet the founders, one of whom was a billionaire on paper while the other two were in the ballpark.

We hit the Museum of Modern Art, Cirque du Soleil, sipped champagne over Janis Joplin's Porsche—heady stuff for a 24-year-old. I was thinking, "Wow, this is something I really want to do for the rest of my life. I want to be a part of this." We rented trucks and went up to Lake Tahoe later in the week (I came crashing back down to Earth after some altitude sickness had me on my knees, vomiting—an ominous portent if I'd been aware at the time.)

The week I started, the company's stock was trading at $88. One year later, it was a penny stock and about 70 percent of the company had been laid off. The dot.com implosion was underway.

Jobless at 24, my career trajectory suddenly changed and I'll never forget the conversation I had with my father after being laid off. He said, "Christopher, this is the best thing that could happen to you. You're young. You're resilient. You don't have a family. You don't have a mortgage. You can do anything you want right now."

My dad had been in the business for many years and had

previously been laid off with a mortgage and a family. He was sort of a career advisor for family, friends, and neighbors, and walked me through it, teaching me how to handle it. He drew me a road map and allowed me to see that the layoff was not the end of the road but rather an opportunity.

People understood that it was no fault of mine, that it was just a seismic period in the dot-com world. And sure enough, I found myself working again before long. A design agency created a business development role for me, which was a blast. The agency produced catalogs for Spiegel and Sears, among other companies.

It was a huge opportunity to accelerate my career and I did well, closing a lot of business and developing my chops.

I spent a year living in London, where I did really well despite a bout of homesickness. After all, I was an Italian kid from New York: I missed my family. I stayed with the company for three years before coming to the conclusion that I was ready to get back into the dot-com world, working in software or tech or digital. But how?

I began interviewing at several places. I gained a lot of traction interviewing with Google, which was very rigorous in its hiring process. I had a total of seven interviews with the company, four or five of which were in person. You would meet with the HR team, who would do two interviews to vet you. Then they would get you into the head of sales, who would vet you, and he would say, "Okay, you can now meet the next in command."

Then, you would have to meet the team, and if they liked you, they'd say, "Great, we think you're okay. We've gotten a good vibe from you. Now we're really going to test you. We're going to give you scripts, and we're going to have you sell our product to an imaginary client. By the way, when you do that, we're going to record the phone call so we can analyze it."

I was in the final stages of this process—the final, final stages. It was down to me and one other person. And I have to admit, I got cocky. Foolishly, I was taking some of these phone interviews at work. I was pretty laid back about it, thinking, "Nobody's going to find out. Besides, I'm going to get this job."

But then, I was suddenly put on probation at work. Now, I don't know this for a fact, but I think it was because they found out I was interviewing for other jobs. I asked my father about his thoughts on the matter and he said, "Yeah, they want you out."

So I didn't go into work the next day. And that's when Google called. Like a knucklehead, I had given them my work number. The receptionist answered and said, "Chris is no longer at the agency." Long story short, I didn't get the job. Google, by the way, went public a few months later.

And to make matters worse, I was fired from the job I did have. Frankly, if I were my boss, I'd have fired me, too: "This kid's taking interview questions at his desk that I'm paying for and on the phone that he should be using to make business development calls for me."

I remember literally lying on my apartment floor as this all soaked in. In a 24-hour period, I had essentially lost two jobs. I also had a new girlfriend (later to become my wife) whom I was falling in love with and wanted to marry.

10 Unique Ways to Immediately Stimulate Your Self-Confidence

I'm not here to patronize you. We know if you walk with better posture, force a fake smile, or get a new haircut, you can trick your brain and boost your self-confidence. Perhaps for 20 minutes you'll think you're the next Richard Branson. I'm here to tell you there are proven ways to improve your self-confidence that will drive real, long-lasting change in your life—*even if you've just lost two jobs.*

1. Meditate

When we feel insecure, it manifests itself in myriad ways. Our bodies don't work. We can't focus. Insecurity creeps when we're not living in the present moment. Taking control of our monkey brain is a profound step toward true self-confidence. I recommend you try the Headspace APP. You can select 5 minute, 10 minute, and 20 minute simple guided meditations.

2. Think inside the box

Having the freedom to make choices with your time can be one of the main reasons why people decide to become entrepreneurs. Too many options can be your downfall. We speak in platitudes that we think carry weight—like "think outside the box." There is a freeing joy in thinking inside the box. Executing on what you know, focusing, and moving the needle are empowering.

3. Learn

The average audio book is 10 hours. If you commute 60 minutes a day, you can listen to about 24 books a year. That's a life changing habit. The more knowledge you have, the greater your confidence will be. Simple. Go and sign up to Audible.com.

4. Teach

If you're an expert in your field, sharing your knowledge will add to your fulfillment as a human being. Feeling fulfilled will add to your confidence. If public speaking terrifies you, consider posting content on platforms like LinkedIn or Medium. Or you can create an online course on Teachable.com.

5. Take Control of Your Career

The best way I know how to do this is to launch your own

personal blog. I recommend the URL be: First name, last name DOT COM. It's a simple notion. If you take control of your personal brand and create content that inspires you, confidence will follow. If you're ready to launch your blog, then you can go to ChristopherDessi.com, where I created a 24-step tutorial that shows you how to do it in 15 minutes.

6. Exercise

Instead of buying expensive clothes, you can work out. Clothes will fit better. Instead of trying to walk with your shoulders back, exercise. Your core muscle strength will enhance your posture and gait. Instead of buying skin products, exercise and hydrate. Your skin will look better. Instead of forcing that fake smile to make you feel happier, exercise. The Mayo Clinic says *"You may also feel better about your appearance and yourself when you exercise regularly, which can boost your confidence and improve your self-esteem."*

7. Get more sleep.

If you have trouble sleeping, try the app called Sleep Cycle. Getting enough sleep helps your brain and body. The Harvard Mental Health Letter states: *"The deepest stage of quiet sleep produces physiological changes that help boost immune system functioning."* The Sleep Cycle app helps you see when you fall into the deepest, most healing stages of sleep. It rouses you with a gentle chime that wakes you at your peak awakeness cycle. Better sleep, sharper mind, better mood, and greater self-confidence.

8. Volunteer | Give Back

I used to volunteer at the Den for Grieving Kids in Green-wich, CT. September 11th happened. My fellow volunteers became my support network. I thought I was giving. I thought I was sacrificing. All the love I could conjure couldn't match the love I felt from that group in the weeks and months after September 11th. Who knows: you may heal someone and you may heal your own soul.

9. Socialize

This can be a difficult one for introverts. Socializing, or finding your tribe, doesn't always have to happen in person. Levering an online community of like-minded people can enhance your self-worth. Abraham Maslow's hierarchy of needs includes belongingness among essential human needs. Contributing on Quora or posting compelling content to your network on LinkedIn can create a real sense of belonging. Similarly, building community via your Twitter account can also stimulate this powerful feeling.

10. Get Curious

Seek people who are more experienced than you. Learning from them will instill a powerful calm of knowing. Chances are, the lessons they share will be invaluable. Most people with "overnight success" stories have experienced trials and tribulations that you may be experiencing. They have all survived and may be able to help you.

I had so many grandiose expectations. In fact, I had already calculated the money I was going to make at Google. Even though it was only a $50,000 a year job—less than I'd been making—I was looking at 10,000 shares of stock just as the company was about to go public, which would vest in four years. I had done the math: a wedding ring the first year, a house the second, and so on.

Your ego just got in the way of the next 15 years of your life, you moron! I told myself. Everything had come crashing down on me. *How had I allowed that to happen?* I wondered.

Meanwhile, my good friends Dave and Amanda were getting married in the next month or two. During my time at the agency, I'd become proficient using iMovie on the company Mac, and I'd promised the happy couple that I'd make them a video as a wedding present. I had quietly been collecting photos of the couple from their family and other friends, putting together little video vignettes on the software program.

Now, despite the rut I was in, I had to put on a happy face and finish the video. The problem was that I had to return the computer to the agency. I talked to Ivan, the IT guy with whom I'd established a good relationship, and begged him to let me keep the Mac another week to finish the video. It felt like insult to injury, sitting over the laptop, shaking as I assembled smiling photos of Dave and Amanda, knowing I had just enough money in the bank to sustain myself for a couple of months and needed to find a new job.

From that painful experience, I realized that if you want to work on building your career, it's important to have reverence for the people who are currently employing you, and work on your own projects on your own time. That may sound self-evident, but as I found out, it's easy to overlook.

In the next job I took, selling email software at a company called Responsys, I was cautious to insulate myself from ever being laid off again. It paid handsomely, allowing me to put away some money to buy an engagement ring, but I wasn't passionate about the work. It just wasn't the right environment for me: too many engineers, not enough sizzle.

In the search for my next career leap, instead of looking at job boards, I began leveraging my network of people to investigate and really dig into businesses. A connection that I had made during my time in London was in the investment banking industry. He would bring me innovative ideas that were ahead of their time. He was the person who introduced me to Netflix, Friendster, and Sirius Radio years before the rest of the world was aware of them. He was also the first person to introduce me to social networking.

I reached out to my old friend and asked, "Where are you investing money?" His bank, TA Associates, had put a lot of cash into a company called Azoogle, an advertising network, and what I now refer to as the grumbling underbelly of the Internet—the teeth-whitening, colon-cleansing, ringtone-getting area of the Internet. That was a realm of the web that I'd never experienced, a very sexy realm in those days, and loaded with money.

I was one of the first three employees in Azoogle's New York office. Oh, man, you talk about getting your hair blown back! We went from 3 people to more than 50 people in less than a year. It exploded. I had a six-figure base salary and within three months, I was pulling in another five figures in monthly commissions. I hadn't even celebrated my 30th birthday.

By this time, I was married with my first child on the way. I'd also been named director of sales, a promotion I basically gave to myself. I decided that I would be taken more seriously and, therefore, sell more if I adopted the title of "director of sales" rather than "sales manager." The boss was fine with it—whatever got us to sell more. I became director of sales, northeast. My two colleagues in the office carved up the rest of the country. It was only on paper, but what the hell? I had advanced my career.

Three years into the job, I was feeling disappointed with the client base—the teeth-whitening, colon-cleansing, ring-tone-getting, grumbling underbelly of the Internet. I wanted bigger brands. I didn't want to be working with the guys at the conference center with the "booth babes" in bikinis; I wanted to work with the big boys. I said to myself, *If I'm a director of sales, I'm good enough to be a vice president of sales.*

I wanted a house in the suburbs, where I could raise a family. I knew I was not going to get there as "director of sales" but as "vice president of sales." The problem? My colleague Brett, who had been hired with me and was one of the company's three directors of sales, had been promoted and was now my boss. And he deserved it; he was amazing at his job. In fact, that was the problem: Brett wasn't going anywhere. There was nowhere for me to go in this company. The only people who knew how good I was at doing my job, apart from me, were my current clients and Brett, and I couldn't exactly go to him and say, "Hey dude, I want your job."

I knew what I wanted. I wanted to become a member of the C-suite. But in the meantime, I was sitting in the general population with my back to the door so that everyone coming in got a nice view of my growing bald spot. It's also where the UPS guy ended up to drop off a package. So now I was the receptionist?

I had to do something to get my career back on track. Having a Master's degree in marketing, meeting with the chief marketing officer seemed a logical step. Maybe I groom myself as a vice president of marketing. So I asked him to lunch. Next, I asked the chief operating officer to lunch. I asked him to be my mentor and asked him if he would meet me on a monthly basis so I could pick his brain. I asked the same thing of the CEO. And they agreed.

I knew to be a part of the C-suite, I needed to learn from these guys. What makes them tick. *What are they missing*, I wondered, *that I could add value to?* I was cocky and ambitious and they were becoming more and more aware of that.

They also saw that I was making $17,000, often $18,000 a month in commissions, on top of my $100,000 base salary. So they brought me into a room and said, "Chris, congratulations. We know you've been looking to advance. We're going to give you a raise to $150,000 a year. Isn't that exciting? But we're going to change your commission structure. Here's how it's going to change and it's effective immediately." They patted me on the back, I shook their hands, and said "Thank you."

Then I went home and did the math. They'd effectively lopped off 30 grand a year from my yearly commissions. They basically wanted to oil the squeaky wheel. They had acknowledged my talent and acted to quiet me down. And I don't blame them. If I had been managing me, I'd have done something similar and said, "Dude, slow your roll. You'll get to the C-suite when you're ready." But I was ambitious. That's why I did the stupid thing I did next.

I had been reading a book by Jack Welch. He explained that to get promoted, you needed to put yourself out there and ask for equal analysis to your peers. That sounded like a good plan. So, for the first time, I went over Brett's head. I went to his boss and said, "Over the next six months, I'd like to have an apples-to-apples comparison with the rest of the sales staff of the quality of clients I bring in, the level of service I bring in, and more of a qualitative analysis as opposed to just the dollars and cents." In quantitative terms, I was already the number-one seller.

I told him I wanted all of that data to be tracked over the next half-year with a guarantee of a promotion to be vice president of sales. Brett's boss asked me to put that request in writing, presumably to make it more official.

Soon after, Brett approached me at my desk with the

printed-out email and asked, "What the [expletive] is this?" He said we needed to talk.

I told him what he already knew, that I just wanted to progress. And although this incident wasn't going to get me axed, my days at Azoogle were numbered nonetheless.

Soon after, I began interviewing. And this was a pivotal moment in the trajectory of my career. I spent $1,000 on a copywriter to clean up my résumé. And she polished it to a shine. I got to thinking, *Wow, this is VP-caliber stuff.* Azoogle was growing at an astronomical rate and I was closing deals left and right.

As a result, I let the headhunters know that I was seeking a vice president of sales position. But they weren't going for it. I was repeatedly offered the director of sales gig with lots of equity at a hot new company as compensation. But I stuck to my guns and said, "I'm not in an equity-type situation right now." At Google, I might have been, but by this time, I needed cash to buy a house and provide for a baby who was on the way.

I kept banging my head on the wall, explaining that, no, I needed to be a vice president of sales. That's when it dawned on me: I needed to write a blog. That's where it all shifted. I realized that if my boss and clients were the only people who understood how good I was, I needed to reach more people. I needed to share my expertise with the world.

As a salesman, you attend a lot of conferences, schmooze a lot of clients—it's a very social thing. I was encountering a lot of guys from other companies. I saw their names popping up in trade publications. They were writing articles about what we were all doing. And I got to thinking, *This guy's a knucklehead. He's a nice guy and all, but man, I don't think he's right. In fact, he's totally wrong. How is he publishing content?*

I asked around and they would say something to the effect of, "Oh, I just reached out to the editor and asked if I could publish the content." So there was no barrier to entry? And by virtue of the industry, neither was there really a hierarchy. At the time, the environment was such that a sales guy could say, "Can I be director of sales?" and the boss would say, "Yeah, you're a director of sales now."

That wouldn't happen on Wall Street. You can't do it that way. You can't have an analyst and say, "All right, you're now a managing director at JP Morgan." It just wouldn't happen that way. There's hierarchy. There's structure. In digital, there's really no hierarchy. I was a corporately bred guy and because of my degrees, I had a corporate mentality. It took a minute for it to dawn on me that this was really the Wild West, that it was really whatever I made of it. I was thinking, *Oh, wow. I can do that, too.*

When I started recognizing names in the trades, I began thinking, *I'm smarter than this guy. Let me show the world that I am.* So I just set up a blog on WordPress and started writing.

My first blog post was about MySpace. I wrote about the fatal flaw of paying for performance, the cost-per-acquisition. I wrote that it was dangerous because you're almost incenting the publisher to do something underhanded and borderline illegal: you're incenting them to make that conversion event happen. What happens if there's a charge-back and a deduction? I was trying to point out that there are very serious FCC regulatory issues involved.

Additionally, what about American Express ads showing up on pornography websites? That happened. Some companies, of course, don't want their brand associated with porn. The AmEx people came to us with the attitude of, "What's wrong with you guys?" But we pointed out that it was generating conversions.

There were a lot of issues like these to write about. And I addressed them on my blog.

When I tell you things happened fast, I mean within a month. The headhunters didn't even peek at my $1,000 resume. They found my articles and began putting me on the interviews I'd been wanting. In those interviews, I'd be asked, "How would you handle that for us? What would you do in this situation or that?"

Something had shifted. All of a sudden, I realized I had found the Holy Grail. My blog had become a repository where these potential new agencies that would hire me were viewing me as a thought leader. My confidence grew. Instead of pandering to them, trying to get $10,000 to $20,000 more just for the title, I came in full swagger. I asked for $100,000 more a year, as well as huge compensation bonuses. I was asking all sorts of crazy demands. And they gave it to me.

But I learned pretty fast that making good money in this line of work puts a target on your back. When it is time for a company to make cuts, you find yourself at the top of the list. After getting clipped from a couple of well-paying gigs, I began casting my net again.

I'll never forget the first time I saw Gary Vaynerchuk speak. He was so passionate about social media, it seemed like he was shot out of a cannon. He electrified the room. I thought, *Okay, I don't have to stay at an ad network. I don't have to be here. I don't have to continue to be an ad network guy and do this one specific job. I want to get into social media.* And that's when I flipped the script and took control of my destiny.

I met with Gary and he advised me to do social before I got into social. What he was telling me was that I needed to find out what I was passionate about and just start talking. I told him I was passionate about being a dad. I started a blog called Dadzilla TV in which I would go on camera and review products for my daughter.

Dadzilla TV gained traction and I felt like I could do this. I figured out how to build a website and I hired a css coder.

I reached back out to Vaynerchuk, who was having a lot of success with his Vaynermedia. I asked if I could come work for him, but he declined, pointing out that I was married with a kid and a mortgage, and he was hiring 22-year-olds right out of college. He couldn't afford me. "Continue to do social and we'll continue talking," he told me.

I still needed to work. I started looking at the venture capital firms to see where the money was going in social media. Then I began checking with the headhunters to see if those companies were hiring. One of those headhunters came back to me and said that there was a role for someone like me at a place called Buddy Media.

They told me they thought I was good but that there was no way they were going to pay me what I was asking. At the time, my base salary was $200K. I told Buddy Media that I wanted $150K. They said, "There's no way we're going to pay you 150. But if you want the job, we'll figure it out."

They had me by the short hairs. I wanted to be excited about joining this company but it meant that I was going to take a hit financially. I had a "Come to Jesus" moment with my wife. I told her that I had to do social media, that this was where my skill set could excel. At this time, I was blogging regularly and I had a strong readership. People were coming to my blog, about 6,000 followers on my Twitter account—a whole ecosystem of people who were listening to me.

I was becoming a real thought leader and drinking the social media Kool-Aid like crazy. Meanwhile, I was making a base salary of $120,000, the least amount of money I'd made in six years, and I didn't care. I was bringing in huge clients: the NHL, Michael Kors, Saks Fifth Avenue. We became the leading software company in social media.

Throughout it all, I was always trying to add value. I looked at the company's Twitter account and thought, *It stinks*. I asked my boss if I could manage it. He told me, "Focus on selling."

"Buddy Media should have a blog," I explained to him.

"Focus on selling," he told me.

I wanted to contribute more to the company than just selling. In hindsight, however, I realize that I probably upset a lot of people. Now that I manage people, I understand that.

The company hired a general manager from Google who arrived there because it had acquired DoubleClick, a competitor of a former company where I had worked. The guy didn't know diddly about social media and, even worse, he thought he did. We didn't hit it off. This was my new boss and I thought, *This is not going to work well.*

One morning, two weeks into this new arrangement, I had a $350,000 contract from Publishers Clearing House that was going to be signed—a nice commission. But an hour before that happened, the CEO pulled me aside. He told me I was being laid off for performance. For performance!? I was stunned. I was speechless. Looking back, I realize I was in the middle of a panic attack. It was like that moment in *Goodfellas* where he thinks he's going to become a "made man" and instead they whack him.

I thought I was going to sign the biggest contract of the day and *boom* I got clipped. There had been nine salespeople at Buddy Media. Eight had been fired over the course of the year. I was the sole survivor. I had worn it like a badge of honor.

I got to my desk and began cleaning it out. The guy from Google said, "You've got to get out of here." I told him I was getting my stuff. I wanted to rip his face off. Someone who knew me, and how good I was at my job, joked, "Chris, spring cleaning?"

"No. I just got fired," I told him.

It got really quiet on the floor. The Human Resources woman was walking me out, and when I finally opened my mouth I was on the elevator. I said, "My wife is pregnant with our second kid. What am I going to do?"

I felt caught with my pants around my ankles. *What just happened?* I wondered. The first thing I remember doing was shooting off a bunch of emails, but not from my company laptop—they had taken that away while I was in the meeting. I didn't have any headhunters in my corner because I had thought I was secure at Buddy Media.

Let me back up for a moment here. This job marked the second time that I'd had my commission structure changed. It was the GM from Google who had raised the issue. I told him I had bought a house in Chappaqua with huge taxes. "This kills me," I told him.

"What is it you want?" he asked. "And how can I advocate for you?" Oh, if I only knew then what I know now.

"Put it in writing," he told me. Yeah, what could go wrong with that?

So I did. I wrote an email, explaining that I would love a 10 percent raise and a better commission structure if they expected me to do what I did. It would also be great, I said, if I could get more responsibility and manage more people. I'd like to advance my career, I added, saying that I thought I could move into management. "I'd like to be a vice president of marketing," I wrote.

In retrospect, I frankly think he had baited the hook and I bit. He passed the email on to the CEO, who was not happy. They offered me two weeks' severance pay. That's it.

Now, I found myself looking for new work and the NHL wanted me. I'd met with everyone and it was a great organization and I was ready to roll when I got word from the man who fired me at Buddy Media. The CEO, his name was Mike, said to me, "It's been brought to my attention that you've been interviewing with competitors, potentially in violation of your non-compete agreement. Therefore, you are no longer eligible for severance."

They didn't even pay me severance.

I spoke to an employment lawyer, who told me that I could fight it but it would likely cost me $20,000 doing so. "Just take it on the chin and leave," he said. So that's what I did.

I had been like a gnat—I just kept coming and coming. I recall the CEO had said something to me as I was asking to tackle social media opportunities. He said, "I think you really want to do your own thing and I encourage you to go and do your own thing."

I see now what I didn't then but that he did: I was an entrepreneur. He was running the company. He didn't need help with that; he needed worker bees.

I didn't realize that I was an entrepreneur at the time because I had always identified myself as being in a sales role. I thrived in that role because I ran my selling like a personal business. I succeeded because I managed myself. I was responsible for my book of business. I managed my clients.

What No One Tells You About Being an Entrepreneur

I've been an entrepreneur for five years. After the first two years, I was broke. I had spent those first two years as an entrepreneur making less money than I had made when I was in my first job out of graduate school. Much less. I had a business partner during those two years. I left him. They call it a "dissolution." I call it a break up.

When the break up was complete, I launched my agency. It was the first time I was 100% on my own. For the first four months, I generated a grand total of $500. My father-in-law had to buy me a laptop. I borrowed money from him to pay my mortgage. My wife was supporting our family. Then something happened.

Salesforce acquired Buddy Media (the company who had fired me two years prior). This was an important event because I was smart enough to buy my small bit of vested equity on my way out the door. I was going to make money. I had gotten lucky.

When I received the check from Buddy Media, I dropped to my knees and wept in the foyer of my home. I pulled myself up to sit on the steps and stared at the check. With tears dripping down my face, I swore that I'd never find myself in that position ever again. It embarrassed me that I cried. But I did. Like a baby. I took that money and leaned into my agency. We hired, closed deals, and got into office space. I had no idea what I was doing. It was terrifying.

My father was deteriorating from ALS, a terminal and brutal disease. It tore his body apart. I would self medicate and drink myself numb every night. Scotch. I couldn't believe he was dying. I would wake up hung over every morning and drag myself into the office. I should have been skipping into the office.

Every day for the past five years, I thought my dad was going to die. He finally did. Every day for five years, I thought my clients were going to fire us. They finally did. Every day for five years, it terrified me that I wouldn't make payroll. I finally missed it. Entrepreneurship? Torture.

It's been horrible.

And amazing.

And then horrible again.

And then amazing again.

I've miscalculated, misinterpreted, and stumbled my way through being an entrepreneur. Sometimes it's been amazing fun. Other times I've hated running my agency more than going to work at the worst jobs I've ever had. Like the time a star employee resigned. Or the time I had to fire another employee. I remembered how it felt to get fired. I didn't want to fire someone. That sucked.

We grew over 3,000% in our second year. I had no idea how to manage that kind of growth. Nor did I know how to manage people. I was a career sales and marketing executive. I knew how to manage myself. I'm learning that managing people means that you don't manage people. That took a while.

I'm horrible at dealing with bad clients. I call it my kryptonite. I fall to pieces. I take it personally. When I get shitty emails from clients, I take it out on my wife or my colleague John. I think they've both become numb to it.

Every summer for the past three years, a huge client event has happened while I've been on vacation. It's become a joke in the office.

- The first time I was in the San Francisco Zoo with my in-laws, wife, and kids. A client fired us. But they also locked us out of their social media accounts and tried not to pay us. I had to spend two hours writing emails, making calls, and cleaning up the carnage. That sucked. We got our money. I had to pay a lawyer. Entrepreneur!

- The second time, last summer, we closed a huge deal. Amazing! We had a skeleton crew because it was smack in the middle of summer. I spent the whole vacation week doing client work. My daughters cried. Entrepreneur!

- The third time, this past summer, as I prepped for vacation, my team joked about our two year bad streak. I got to the airport and the first email I checked was from a client firing us. I had to excuse myself from my family and take a walk around JFK to calm down, leaving my wife alone with our daughters. I spent two hours composing the perfect response. I salvaged the relationship (for now). Entrepreneur!

I've produced four globally-recognized events in three years. I lost a lot of money on those events. So did my partners. I'm a slow learner. I won't be producing any more events.

I appear on television. It's fun. They never pay me. I study, take time away from my business, put makeup on my face, and blabber for four minutes. I used to call my Dad after every appearance. He loved it. Now he's gone, and I'm not sure why I still go on TV. I've closed one deal in five years as a direct result of those appearances. It was the worst client I've ever had. I think she wanted to sleep with me. The last time we spoke, she screamed and hung up on me.

I wrote a mediocre book. I thought that's what entrepreneurs did. It shot to #1 on Amazon's hot new releases and then it stopped selling. When I speak at conferences and mention my book, I show a photo of a pretty girl instead (better to look at the girl than buy the book, I tell them).

Then I wrote another book (this one). Like I said, I'm a slow learner.

I have nightmares about missing payroll again. My CMO and I have elected not to pay ourselves twice to ensure we don't miss payroll a second time. I haven't saved a dime in the past five years. Everything I make gets poured back into the agency.

Last year, I lost two of my biggest clients on the same day. What are the odds? At least one had the decency to call me. I thought I was going to have a heart attack. I sat in the conference room in the dark for hours.

In the past five years that I've been an entrepreneur, I've visited the ER three times because I thought I was having a heart attack. They were most likely panic attacks. That may have had something more to do with my dad being sick, but there I was in the ER nonetheless.

I had to learn how to meditate so I didn't assume I was dying every time I lost a client.

I'm learning. I have doubt. I often refer to experts to help guide me. I have so much to learn. Sometimes I don't refer to experts and I mess up. Sometimes I feel like I'm about to take a huge final and the teacher won't tell me what's on the test. All I want to know is what to study.

I'm a voracious reader (listener?). I listen to audiobooks. Sometimes I get frustrated when I read/listen to books. I would read a book and have more questions than when I started it. So I decided to reach out to the thought leaders and dig deeper. Now I have a "Success Feature" on my blog. It takes a ton of time. I should focus more on making money and less on interviewing people. But I'm so curious.

I love public speaking. I used to get in trouble for talking back to my parents when I was kid. Now I get paid to speak. It's great. Nobody interrupts me. People are nice. I get to tell people what I know and what I see as truth. I'm good at it. Sometimes I hate social media. I run a social media agency. I don't have a million twitter followers. Sometimes I feel like the Willie Loman of social media.

It sucks being an entrepreneur. Sometimes I feel like I'm Robin.

But it's also phantasmagorically awesome, because today I'm Batman.

It was a little bit like being thrown out of the nest when you really like the nest. It was a plush little nest and I wanted acknowledgment for trying to add beautiful twigs to it and help shape it. Meanwhile, the boss was like, "Shut up, I'm trying to hatch all these other eggs over here—get the hell out of my nest." He had correctly identified me as an entrepreneur.

I thought, "Okay, I can do this on my own."

That experience did something to me. Never again, I vowed, would I be vulnerable to someone else's ability to take away my livelihood. I felt like a loser. I got a little bit angry. I got focused. I would no longer ask for permission to take control of my fate.

As a result, I now run my own company, Silverback Social; I'm a frequent guest on Fox TV; and I'm making a financially rewarding living doing what I'm meant to do. The promise of this book is that you can do the same in your life.

SO HERE'S THIS AMAZING THING—THE INTERNET—FOR BUILDING YOUR BRAND

"Driving an active social presence for your brand is critical to a successful business. In my mind, social is now one of the most pivotal aspects of brand development and engagement with new prospects and customers. Social isn't one element of marketing; it is embedded across every element. As an executive, you should be an active spokesperson and authority for your brand."

— TAMI CANNIZZARO, HEAD OF
MARKETING, EBAY ENTERPRISE

WHETHER YOU LIKE IT OR NOT, SOCIAL MEDIA IS happening to your brand.

Let me explain what I mean with an example. I love Breitling watches. I have a Breitling watch that I bought with a small inheritance that I got from my grandfather. Instead of doing the frugal thing and putting the money in a bank, I decided I wanted something to remind me of my papa. I bought a Breitling watch, which I've had for years now. Right before I step onto a stage, I touch it and I think of Papa. It's a wonderful piece of man jewelry.

When I started at Buddy Media, I knew that I wanted to work with brands that I thought were cool. I worked with the NHL, the Philadelphia Eagles, and Michael Kors—these are cool, interesting brands. I went to Connecticut and met with Breitling's executives. I gave my social media spiel and they said, "Chris, this is all very well and good but we don't do social media. We're a luxury brand."

That was discouraging. I immediately opened my laptop and searched "Breitling" on Facebook. What do you think I found? I found there was a Facebook page with 32,000 fans. Their marketing officer quickly shot a look at the vice president of marketing, then to the director of corporate communications. Then she said, "That's not us."

"No kidding."

The guy running the page was from Jordan and was probably selling counterfeit watches but he was telling the world that he was Breitling.

Some time later, I emailed the CEO of Breitling and said, "You should know that I use you as a negative example in all of my speeches. If you want me to consult for you, I'd be more than happy to take the meeting."

He explained that he was well aware of my example and that the company was now very active in social. They recovered from it. A brand should have a voice and be in charge of what it is saying.

"People want a human connection with a company" John Hall, CEO of Influence & Co., told me. His business was ranked number 72 on *Forbes'* list of "America's Most Promising Companies."

Hall explained that people need to trust you and your brand and "one of the best ways they can do that is through reading your content. I can tell you from my personal experience that business opportunities consistently come to us at Influence & Co. through my published content. And it not only brings us opportunities, but it makes me a better leader by challenging me to stay ahead of the game."

He said he was sure that some companies could survive without generating and publishing content, but added, "However, it's become such an essential part of differentiating your company and leading your industry that I'd highly recommend all business leaders generate valuable thought leadership content."

"A borderless audience" is the way that Startup Buenos Aires founder Lisa Besserman describes digital media. She says it "allows missions to become movements, and words to become actions." She also points out that the reach and impact of digital media, social networks, and online communities make it possible to work with and connect global startup ecosystems.

Back in 2009, social media was essentially a tool for companies to build their brands. Today, individuals realize that they are publishers and that they, too, are brands in and of themselves.

I recently asked John Dokes, AccuWeather's Chief Marketing Officer, about digital media. He said "It has been and continues to be a critical part of building unique, close brand relationships with audiences" and that it has also allowed him to "see a quicker return on ideas and tests that used to take years," adding that it is an ideal tool for marketers and innovators.

Dokes gets it in a way that most people don't. I say "most people," but there is an entire generation of people who are better equipped for this technology than the rest of us: the Millennials. It's also true of the generation coming up behind them, people who don't even realize that there was ever a different way of doing things.

These young people don't realize that you couldn't produce an iMovie by using an app, taking video content, and publishing it on YouTube. They don't realize there was another way of doing things, of not publishing. They are natural publishers and natural brands.

In the past, your brand—your reputation—was shaped by your personal interactions. If you appeared on TV or published a book or an article, that was a form of currency for your brand. Today, however, there is exponentially less friction combined with exponentially more control in creating and managing your brand. You need to manage your brand, which does, in fact, exist. You, and anyone else who's looking, will find it online. If you don't, it's not that you don't have a brand—it's actually that you have a very negligible one.

If you don't like what your online presence says about you, then take control of your fate and change it. I've heard speakers at colleges tell students to stay off of social media. The intention is right—don't allow yourself to be seen in a professionally embarrassing light—but not only is the advice unlikely to be heeded, it's just plain wrong. Instead of hiding your presence, I tell students, define your presence.

Imagine there's a photo of you at a party that you just happened to have attended for five minutes. You're completely sober and buttoned-up. However, later in the evening—long after you've left—things got out of hand and the police had to be called. There are embarrassing photos of drunken escapades, which, of course, find their way online. Maybe you were tagged as being at that party.

Now, if you take the advice that says "don't be on social media," then this photo is going to represent a much larger share of your online presence than it should. On the other hand, if you dilute, so to speak, the image by posting 10,000 more photos, photos of you involved in much more virtuous activities, a Google search is much less likely to uncover the potentially embarrassing information.

In other words, don't be a victim of social media by allowing others to cast you in any way they see fit. Instead, take control of your brand by using social media to your benefit, painting yourself as you want the world to see you.

There is a chasm among the generations: Millennials and younger are generating content around them while older people are more involved in its consumption than production. This idea of content creation, however, is seeping into the older generations to the point that people my age now see their friends and families generating content, and although it's not as natural and as organic as it might be for Millennials, it's becoming more and more ingrained.

Women who've been stay-at-home moms are now all over Instagram taking selfies when they go out with their friends, and many have started "mommy blogs," built communities, and even generated income that way.

All of a sudden, there is a cultural phenomenon: individuals who have said "I don't do social media" are now tagged in the photographs, are now having blog posts written which include them, and are now part of the corporate communications press release because they are at the company barbecue where the CEO is tweeting because he knows it has an effect on his stock price.

Whether they intended to be a part of that or not, it is

happening to them. Eventually, there's a moment of clarity in which a person decides, "Either I am in it or I'm going to be eaten by it."

For the people who don't like it, well, people didn't like it when Elvis got on stage and wiggled his hips. My grandparents hated it when the Beatles came around and girls screamed at the top of their lungs. They hated the Rolling Stones. My dad hated Axl Rose, who had long hair and jailhouse tattoos all over his arm. Now, that's considered Classic Rock.

"If you're working for someone who doesn't get social or see the value, I would be concerned they aren't a forward-thinker in marketing." That's from Tami Cannizzaro, Head of Marketing at eBay Enterprise. "If your boss sees social as a boondoggle," she goes on, "don't throw caution to the wind. Tone it down. Or better yet, find a new boss." And she's not kidding. She advises to take a risky job before it is too late, as it becomes harder later in life.

There will always be naysayers. Well, too bad. Things change. Social media impacted businesses, but businesses got it—some a little bit later than others. Now, the same thing is happening to people and they need to understand it.

These days, we have these platforms that have become ubiquitous within business and especially in corporate America. I'm thinking of LinkedIn. People network in corporate America via LinkedIn and it's just the way it is. It's perfectly acceptable. There are CEOs on LinkedIn as well as first-year employees.

But when the site was still new, people got nervous and would tell me things like, "If I create a LinkedIn profile, my boss is going to think I'm looking for a job," under the impression that it was just an online résumé.

LinkedIn has been around long enough now so people understand that that's not what it's about. It's about having a personal brand. It provides you the ability to publish content and flex your intellectual muscles. That doesn't require you to be completely self-serving, though. You can talk about the great things that your organization does.

The site has algorithms that allow good content to rise to the top. The exciting part is that you have the ability for 30,000 people to read that content because if it's good stuff, it gets read. If it's not, it won't get read—and that's fine, too.

I always encourage people to blog and the easiest first step is publishing on LinkedIn. Check with your boss and see what the parameters are. Ask if you're allowed to publish content. Explain that you'll be appropriate in what you write, avoid giving away trade secrets, adhere to checks and balances, and clear everything through Human Resources if asked.

Whatever your expertise within the company, this is your opportunity to display it, with one goal being to drive new business back to the website. Additionally, you should be reading other experts' blogs. Maybe you've written something similar or something relevant to the topic. In that case, you can post a link to yours with an explanation of its relevancy.

By doing so, you're not being a jerk and just saying, "Here, read my blog"; you're actually providing context. What you're saying, in essence, is: "I read your blog post and found it really interesting. I wrote something similar to that." Now you have another link to your content.

Suppose you post just three to five times a year. If you have a 3,000-person organization and you've got 1,000 people publishing 3 to 5 times a year, you've got a lot of content. And that's a heck of a lot better than spending money on press releases. Instead, you've got the people who are actually in the organization buoying everything that the organization does from one social outlet.

Now, imagine if each of those individuals was trained on how to leverage Twitter, LinkedIn, and other social media sites. Imagine if they had their own personal blogs and they were generating content by commenting and sharing on their colleagues' LinkedIn profiles and blogs, with back links, which navigate back to the organization.

This is search engine optimization at its best, most organic, and most powerful. And it doesn't cost the company a dime. It's all about sweat equity. You just allow your community to be brand advocates on your behalf and it all links back to your website.

People say, "Oh, that sounds so exhausting." Maybe so, but there are worse things than fatigue. There's anonymity, for one thing. If you don't put in the effort, then another business is going to be indexed higher on Google. Maybe you fall to the second page or lower. Might as well be Siberia. Why not train your team and get everyone excited about generating content?

"But Chris," you say, "we're not very good writers." Who cares? There are tools that you can use to fix that. For starters, install the Hemingway app on every machine in your organization. The app ranks your writing with a score, which tells you what grade level you're writing at—fourth grade, fifth grade, etc. The app will advise you on how to write clearer sentences that can be easily digested by your readers.

Dave Kerpen, a successful company founder and CEO, told me that writing has been critical to his success.

"Writing has helped me to become a better thinker, which in turn has helped me to become a better leader," Kerpen said. "I try to write simply and concisely, and I like to tell stories. If my kids can read a LinkedIn post of mine, that's a good thing."

There are other tools that can make this part of the job easier as well. There is software called CoSchedule, for instance. Suppose you have a company blog and some old but still-relevant content. This will allow you to re-leverage that old content, scheduling days in which you will repost that material.

Understand that repetition is necessary in social media. Just because you tweet something, that's not the end of it. Of course, it's likely to be retweeted by others and shared through various networks. But two weeks down the line, you should, assuming it's still relevant, repost that tweet. It might then reach entirely new audiences who had not seen the initial tweet. Six weeks down the line, eight weeks, keep it up.

And this is where something like CoSchedule becomes so handy, because the software schedules these retweets and blog re-posts so that content is automatically pinging out on a regular basis.

This is what you should be doing regardless of whether or not you like your job. It's something you should be doing if you're running or planning to start your own business. Realistically, you are running your own business, your own brand, because, after all, there are no guarantees in this life. Maybe you'll retire having only worked one job for 50 years. Probably not, but it doesn't matter. You give yourself leverage and you prepare yourself for eventualities by building your brand.

WHAT IT MEANS TO BUILD YOUR BRAND AND WHY YOU SHOULD DO IT ACTIVELY

"Your brand identity is one of your greatest assets, and it's what will drive opportunities to you and to the company you represent. As long as you build and maintain a strong, positive brand for yourself, there will always be opportunities for you whether you're an experienced executive, an entrepreneur getting your business off the ground, or a student just starting out."

— JOHN HALL, CEO, INFLUENCE & CO.

WHEN I SPEAK ABOUT SOCIAL MEDIA, I OFTEN PIGGY-back off a Ted Talk given by Clay Shirky some years ago. He pointed out that over the past 500 years, there have been just a few major inventions that have changed the culture and the way that we aggregate and disseminate information. And he begins by discussing the printing press.

Prior to the printing press, information was largely exchanged face to face. You got information, you walked down the street, you passed that information along to another person. All of a sudden, information was being disseminated at a much faster rate and traveling much further. Propagandists and advertisers suddenly wielded far more influence. Newspapers eventually came along and took the printed word to new and greater heights.

And then there was a shift from the one-to-many model to the one-to-one model when the telephone was invented. And after that, people were able to bridge vast distances across the planet and communicate privately. Previously, we had exchanged information from village to village and with this invention, information can be shared globally.

Radio and television eventually come on the scene and people are then able to experience a shared experience in real time. These media provide social experiences as people gather to listen and watch.

And now, there's the Internet. The Internet is a catch-all for all of the previous media inventions over the last 500 years. Weave them all together—the printing press, mail delivery, telephones, radio, movies, television—and now you have social media.

What that means is that no longer do you have to go to an editor to write about your business or to sell your propaganda or to tell your story because now you can create a blog and publish it yourself for the world to see.

No longer do you go to a radio station and say, "Please tell my story" or "Please advertise my company, Mr. Radio Station Man." Now you can simply start your own podcast. No longer do you have to go to a book publisher to print your novel or to a TV station or a movie studio to create your filmed entertainment because now there is YouTube, Vimeo, Vine, and Instagram video. The gates have been torn down and the gatekeepers, who once were necessary to gain access, are gone. That is what social media has done. It has taken the power, once held tightly in the hands of the few, and dropped it right into every individual's lap.

I begin every speech to senior executives that way. The reason I do is because whenever I say "social media" to execs, they immediately assume I am just talking about Facebook and Twitter, and they reactively shake their heads and groan.

The idea I want to get across is that businesses, just like individuals, are more empowered than ever before in history, and that these tools are free to leverage. I'm reminded of a dog accustomed to a wire fence in a backyard that has become so classically conditioned to the parameters provided by that wire fence that it takes those boundaries for granted. With the tools of social media, there is no wire fence. That dog can run free wherever it pleases but it first has to realize that as a possibility.

I find this example of empowerment to be a great starting point as I explain social media to others. It took me a while to figure out the possibilities even as I was working in the industry. Because we are so used to being conditioned to look up to others to tell us what to do and provide us with guidance, it can be difficult to take the reins for ourselves.

The entire world is utterly flat. There is zero hierarchy. That hierarchy only lives and breathes in your own mind. You have control of your destiny. You are able to tell your story as you see fit. It's not simply about posting on Facebook or tweeting; instead, by virtue of empowering yourself by presenting your own content, you are able to curate the *you* that you aspire to be.

That's a lot to digest. There is, however, an easy place to begin. There is a very simple way to find out what your brand currently looks like. It's this: Google yourself.

To be fair, that's a bit of a scare tactic I use when I'm training executives. It shouldn't really be scary, but maybe it should be a little bit scary. Because the reality is that if you're not consciously managing your online identity, you have no idea what you actually look like to the rest of the online world. Social media is no longer a choice and the people who are leveraging it no longer even consider it to be social media as much as the natural progression of the information-gathering process, so much so that "Googling" is now just part of the vernacular.

When I was a kid—not to digress too far here, but—I would ask my parents questions and they would tell me to "go look it up." My mother was an educator, so that was a natural and wholly appropriate response, and it was fun. We would sit down with a dictionary or encyclopedia and literally look up the answer to my question. Now people say, "Google it."

The repercussions of this idea are thrilling but, at the same time, can be quite terrifying. Consider sending in your résumé for a job. A potential employer has 500 résumés stacked on his desk. Once that number has been whittled down to a list of the most appropriate candidates for the position, what is that person going to do next? Google you. And when they Google your name, what will they find?

If that employer doesn't see a positive, appropriate, and compelling portrait of you above the fold—that has not been purchased through Google Ads, mind you—you're automatically behind the eight ball. And needlessly. It's such an easy process to create this portrait that if you haven't taken this basic step, that person has to ask, "How much do you really want the job?"

To simply be competitive, you need to create an appropriate LinkedIn page. And then start to blog on it or, if you prefer, create your own blog on WordPress. By doing this, you automatically are generating content around your name. That content goes beyond just your Facebook page or just your Twitter account, which just about everyone in the world has by this point.

Your blog is evidence of your professional content curation. I call it one's digital posture. When someone Googles you, whatever comes up is their first impression of you. Their second impression of you is what they find when they then click on you. And now the danger is that what they see is a Facebook page that doesn't have the appropriate privacy settings implemented and so the world sees you with a lampshade on your head doing something stupid.

On that note, the idea of "frictionless" bears mentioning. I recall an incident in which an EMT worker posted some run-of-the-mill complaints about the job on her Facebook page. It's not something uncommon at all, but I remember this particular situation because it cemented for me the dangers of a medium that becomes an extension of our personal discourse. And Facebook and Twitter have become just that—private or semi-private conversations that happen publicly in broad daylight, so to speak.

The woman was complaining as people on social media are wont to do, but her crucial mistake was that she referenced the company that employed her. She didn't tag the company— she merely mentioned it in passing as she vented to friends. Someone spotted it. You just never know who among your network of friends has stronger allegiances to people other than you. The post made its way back to the company and she was fired.

One of the things we do at Silverback Social is to write social media privacy and compliance parameters for businesses and organizations so that if an employee posts something negative toward the company on a social media platform, the company is well within its rights to terminate that person. This is not only a serious issue but it's one that is going to get worse and worse. It's also going to get muddier and muddier over time. The reason is because the social networks have become almost frictionless, meaning when something happens, people take a photo and post it without even considering the repercussions of what will happen as a result of that photo.

Facebook went from being a platform used mainly in colleges at first that eventually extended into organizations. I was an early adopter within my age demographic because I was out of college and I am naturally an early adopter and I'm in the industry. I'm a digital marketer and digital marketers test out every new tool that they think that they can market to individuals.

After a few years, others joined in. And one day, all of our grandparents are on Facebook. The reason why grandparents are on is because they want to see pictures of their grandchildren and great-grandchildren. The ubiquity of Facebook has gotten to the point where everybody you know is on it, unless they proactively opted out of it because of privacy concerns, which I absolutely love, admire, and respect. Do what you want to do. Opt out of it if you like.

The majority of people in your life likely have a Facebook profile. Maybe they don't use it that often, maybe they're on it all the time, maybe they're on it too much. But the idea is that because it has become a cultural phenomenon and because people expect to see certain types of postings on Facebook, the parameters that we previously used to guide our instincts have now loosened.

Even a year ago, most people probably wouldn't have been comfortable posting a selfie. But because selfies have become so ubiquitous and because Ellen DeGeneres shot a selfie with a bunch of movie stars during the Oscars, people began to think *Oh, selfies are cool. Everybody's posting a selfie* whereas previously they might have felt self-conscious, afraid of being perceived as being too self-involved. But when everybody is doing the self-involved thing of taking a photograph of themselves, then it becomes the norm, and because it is the norm, the idea of what is appropriate or inappropriate becomes blurred.

While even the amount and frequency of posting content has become blurred, the appropriateness of content has become downright cloudy. Things that used to be private—disputes, bodily functions, funerals (not kidding)—are now routinely documented for public consumption. Today, if the hassle of actually holding an iPhone up and touching a button to take video is too strong, we have GoPro cameras, for example, which are affixed to clothing or headwear to free up hands while life is recorded without any thought about what is being filmed.

Not only is a whole generation growing up fully immersed in this frictionless new world, but our entire society is doing the same thing, feeling perfectly comfortable documenting everything in their lives. And I don't mean just what they had for lunch. I mean whatever is happening at work, at home, in their social lives. We're about to the point where if you don't post a dinner with you and your wife that night, it didn't happen. If you don't post a photograph of yourself at a party, you weren't there. If you don't post video of a vacation, it certainly didn't happen.

When this shift toward frictionless began to happen, the boundaries of appropriateness became blurred, which is dangerous. Five years ago, an EMT being fired over a Facebook post was news. Now it's not news because people get fired every single day for posting on social media.

As I mentioned previously, I spend a lot of time talking to college students about this, challenging them to rethink much of the advice they've been given about not posting. It is completely unrealistic. I try to teach people that, when they post, they should be conscious about it.

I also encourage people to be diligent about monitoring their presence online. Just because *you* are conscious about what you post doesn't mean everyone else is: again, frictionless. Not everyone engages in embarrassing activities at parties, I understand, but even a straight-arrow student who gets all A's might still be tagged in a photo at the beach in a bikini or with visible tattoos. It's not that there is anything wrong with that; it's simply not the first thing that a potential employer should learn about you when considering you for a job.

As Jim Treacy puts it, "If you don't define yourself, somebody else will do it for you." And whether you think that's right or wrong, that's just the nature of the way the world works.

The flip side of that is that if you've been generating content for the past four years—blogging about your studies or how you pay for tuition, photos of your travels or sporting events, whatever—that is constructing a different and more carefully managed persona. Now, you're 10 steps ahead of the game. You're demonstrating a lot of skills, the most basic and maybe important of which is the ability to present a positive image.

The question one has to ask, because it is so simple, is, "Why wouldn't you manage your digital posture?"

Attorney Russ Adler understands this concept as well as anyone. His message is simple: "Value your reputation above all else." He says of reputation that it is "the most important currency you have as a professional."

If you're an entrepreneur looking to raise money, nobody is going to give it to you unless you have an appropriate business connection of some kind. If you have no online footprint, people will probably wonder if you are who you say you are or if there's a sinister reason for your anonymity or if you are some sort of con artist.

And for those people who say they don't care what Google has to say about them, and that they'll be just fine when they get to sit down face to face with another human being, I tell them not to shoot the messenger. Google is everyone else's close, trusted friend. And if Google says you're a lampshade knucklehead, no amount of handshaking and eye contact is going to convince them that underneath it all, you're not just that same old knucklehead in the photo. That's just how it is.

To get a sense of what this brave new world means, let me remind you what selling was like in the old days. When I started out selling, I was basically able to make a sell because of my relationships. I didn't realize that I was in sales. I started as an account manager. I built relationships and I started selling when I wasn't even trying to sell. However, as I got bigger jobs and I had to really sell, it came down to cold calling and trying to get as much information about the individual or company as I possibly could. And in those early days of this century, that meant using the telephone.

Part of the dreaded cold call is that there were gatekeepers. For example, there was always a secretary. Once you got the secretary, you had to leave a compelling message. You had to have a compelling call to action. Then, you would try hooks. I remember Jeffrey Gitomer had a book called *Jeffrey Gitomer's Little Red Book of Selling*. It was full of hooks like, "Bob's name came up in conversation this morning. I'd like to talk to him about it."—things that would be compelling so individuals would call you back.

That was a very difficult and arduous line of work which required calling 100 people in a 3-day period. I used to set a bar for myself that I would make at least 15 calls a day no matter what. That sounds easy—15 sounds like a small number. In reality, that is a huge pain in the neck. And if you realize that it's already 3:00 p.m. and you have busy work to get done still and you haven't made those calls, you're in trouble.

I'd make my calls after noon, for the most part, because busy executives were usually in meetings in the mornings. So I'd spend my time trying to do as much research as I could prior to that. And lo and behold, I began to discover that there was information out there online. Some companies had websites. Some of those websites had blogs. And then there was LinkedIn, where executives even had profiles.

It was still the early days of the site, so there was that stigma that if you had an account, you were looking for a job. But that began to change. And as a result, the information that you had been looking for—that you had been digging for—was now being spoon-fed to you. These companies were and are giving away the information. They're telling you what they're paying attention to. They're telling you what their annual report looks like. They're telling you about new hires. All through a LinkedIn press release.

Meanwhile, they're also having multiple internal conversations back and forth as well as conversations with the public. They have corporate content and CEO blogs. They're posting about corporate events. Bottom line: you now have all these different opportunities to connect with these people on a completely different level.

But to get the attention of these people, you need to have an online presence as well. When you begin generating content of your own, you will make a first impression. And then, someone will click on you and you'll get that second impression. And once they see your content and realize that maybe you are credible, you're much more likely to have calls returned to you and in an expeditious fashion. Radio/TV host and author Jeff Hayzlett understands this. In fact, he told me that he uses

LinkedIn, in addition to Twitter, Facebook, and Instagram, to not only engage audiences but also to sell products.

"This is the new way of selling," Hayzlett explained. "Business leaders need to understand that their community is online and if you want to reach them, you need to be there, too. That's what social media is about—engaging with an audience that is interested in your company."

Nothing is harder than shooting out of the gate and trying to sell somebody something when that person doesn't know anything about you. But if you can position yourself as a thought leader, that changes things.

Suppose you're a real estate agent, for instance. You can spend your time cold calling or you can spend that time posting about local real estate trends, tips for new home-buyers, or some other content that provides value to others. Now, when others Google you, they will determine that you're legitimate. And the Internet, which was previously something of a gatekeeper for you, is now opening the gate as well as the front door. This, I believe, is the future of selling.

For people who still think that voicing your opinion on matters is too risky, I say rethink that. People have asked me whether they should talk about their religious affiliation. Absolutely, talk about that. They say things like, "Well, I might not get clients because maybe they're Jewish and I'm a gentile."

If they are Jewish and they are heavily involved in their synagogue, they are likely going to have even more reverence for you because you are heavily involved in your church. And that also means that you are both spiritual people and that if you are going to do business together, that person is probably going to have a greater amount of trust in you because of the moral code that religion requires—in which case, you may be exactly the type of person that like-minded people want to do business with. And if someone does have prejudices against you for your religious beliefs, why would you want to work with that person to begin with?

By providing content about your values, you are automatically curating the list of people who are interested in talking to you. Furthermore, you also cut through a lot of small talk later on. You save people a lot of time trying to get to know you because you've already told them a lot of that initial information. Assume going into any meeting that the others in the room have already Googled you and, accordingly, know who you are.

I walk into a room knowing that if somebody Googled me, he or she has gotten the propaganda that I put out. It's the Chris Dessi who met his future father-in-law for the first time, who sits on set at CNN, who runs a marathon by himself for ALS. Is that me all the time? Of course not. But it's the guy I want to cultivate for practical purposes. And when you know that you're in charge of crafting that persona, you carry a little extra confidence around in your back pocket.

When people know you before you sit down—the *you* that you designed—it puts them a little bit more at ease and allows you to refrain from doing all the talking. If you don't have to sell yourself to everyone, you can spend that time listening or asking questions. You can relax. If, on the other hand, your personal digital brand is not air-tight, you will have to sweat it out, anxious as to whether or not they dug up something about you that might come back to bite you in the rear.

A sales executive I once advised explained to me that he had an arrest on his record dating back to college. He said that the incident was the very first thing that popped up on a Google search of him. *There are things you can do about that*, I told him. There are "black hat" ways to push that material down but I told him I didn't recommend that because Google can penalize you for that if they find out you're doing it. If, however, you organically generate good content in a consistent manner, appropriate to what you're focusing on, the results will naturally push down the negative content. It isn't an overnight process, I explained, but that it would take some time and effort. It's a chipping-away process.

So now you might be wondering what your brand actually looks like—or should look like. What should you actually include and what should you exclude as you build this digital posture? I have empathy for people who are diving into this and think, *Oh, my. You want me to talk about everything?* My advice is to talk about what you are comfortable with sharing.

When I first began, I didn't know what to say. Over time, I realized that the more authentic I was, the more engaged my audience was regardless of whether it was on Facebook, LinkedIn, or Twitter. It doesn't matter what the subject matter is. Just be real. Let your personality seep through. There is an enormous amount of noise out there that is competing with your brand, along with highly managed paid content, so the more that people connect with what you have to say, the more others will find you.

Another reason to allow your personality to shine is because the more authentic people who find you, the more credibility you acquire as a thought leader. Suppose you are really passionate about *Star Wars*. If you are, then you should be writing about it. As Gary Vaynerchuk put it, "If you're into Smurfs, Smurf it up." People freak out about sharing something so personal, as opposed to professional, but there is good reason to do it.

As a result of your sharing about your personal passions, you'll extend your network of readers. If you are able to marry your love of *Star Wars* with your professional life—say, by drawing business principles from the Jedi code—you're going to connect with both a business audience and that *Star Wars* crowd as well. It not only grows your audience but also makes you a more relatable person because everyone has hobbies and passions apart from work.

This thing that is social media is more of a spiritual awakening than a technological one. What I mean is that we are connecting as human beings in a way that we never have before, and it is a more authentic way of communicating. To get a glimpse of this, consider the way that LinkedIn profiles used to read: they would say something like: "Chris Dessi is an entrepreneur." They would use the third-person voice despite the fact that everyone knows that I'm the one writing this stuff. Now, we write, "My name's Chris and I'm an entrepreneur." The first-person voice is so much more genuine, isn't it?

In a way, the digital world is just like real life in that the more comfortable you get being sincere with others, the more they will become comfortable with you and trust you.

Two of the most trafficked blogs I've ever written will illustrate this principle. The first was about the captain of my rugby team in college, Sean Lugano, who was killed in the terror attack of September 11th. I wrote the post on the 10th anniversary of the attack to express how terrible it was that my friend had been murdered. I was now happy, had a great home, a beautiful wife, and two wonderful children. I was thrilled with my life and it got me very upset because Sean never got to do this. And now, as a parent myself, it dawned on me what Sean's parents must have gone through and what agony they must still be feeling.

I wrote that blog post to get those feelings off my chest but as a byproduct of that post, I closed deals. I would walk into board rooms and guys would have tears in their eyes. They would share about friends that they, too, had lost on 9/11.

Once again, we're not talking about business. We're not talking about my résumé. We're not talking about how I'm going to raise money or what my asking price is. Nobody is selling anything. We're real people talking about real life, and all because I was secure enough to write my thoughts in a blog and share it with others.

Again I can turn to Dave Kerpen, who sums it up well: "Transparency is actually quite freeing, and a great differentiator. Most people are afraid to be radically transparent. So if you can open up and share your heart, people will respond to that." That's the truth.

The other blog post that resonated incredibly well with people was one I simply titled: "I'm a Loser." In it, I told the story that I shared above about being laid off three times in two years. I explained that because I have those scars and have had to reinvent myself again and again, I am a much better executive. Rather than getting comfortable in the same job for 15 years, I've had to learn new tricks every step of this entrepreneurial journey.

That post scared the heck out of me. I wondered if it was appropriate to talk about. I wasn't sure if I should mention killing a bottle of scotch by myself after getting laid off. Or about the pain that made me feel, well, like a loser. But I posted it. The outreach was absolutely overwhelming because, guess what: 9 times out of 10, somebody you know has also been laid off and somebody you know is going to admire the fact that you were brave enough to write a blog post and share that. I never lost a deal because I was honest about the experiences that I had. In fact, it has only landed me more deals.

Relationships happen when you and the person sitting across from you connect as human beings. The moment you can be a touch self-deprecating or you can stop taking yourself so seriously, you become tighter with that person, and it expedites the entire relationship. And that's when good things start to happen.

Part of the reason that I wrote the "I'm a Loser" post is because I had been through it and was now on the other end. I wanted other people going through it to understand that the sun would still come up the next day and that opportunities would soon arrive. And when you generate content from a genuine place in order to do good, the magic begins. Things you never conceived of find their way to you.

I had been under the assumption that I was only writing a blog, aiming to get my content out there in order to be a thought leader in my industry with the eventual aim of landing that elusive vice president job. But one day, a producer found my content and put me on TV. Now, I'm a talking head. That's something I never even imagined I would be doing. I didn't even know I wanted to. But that's what happens when you put your ideas out there for the world to see. Your opportunities will expand when you stop thinking of yourself as a person who works for this company or that and simply begin thinking of yourself as your own brand.

I'm certainly not saying go out and quit your job and start your own company. Don't leave that security, if that's a psychological security for you, but what I am saying is the real security is having liquid cash in the bank. Having a 9-to-5 job is not real security, as we've all seen. Jobs are shipped overseas, replaced by cheaper labor or even automation.

Maybe you work for a company that turns out to be involved in a scandal. If you've been the guy for 15 years doing the same thing at Enron, for example, and Enron disappears, you are a white elephant. And if you don't have a digital brand identity, you are a worst-case scenario because nobody knows who you are except for that company that just imploded. Nobody cares that you were political enough to work your way up that hierarchical ladder.

What can you do? You can start today to insulate yourself from that. And you can do it while you're doing your 9-to-5. This message I have is not to make you feel warm and fuzzy about self-improvement. It is a call to arms. I'm telling you because everything could go away tomorrow.

THE SEVEN PILLARS OF YOUR BRAND

"Success is when you have reached a pinnacle of what you set out to do that you can begin to teach others."

— SHEILA HAILE, CHIEF MARKETING OFFICER, COHEN'S FASHION OPTICAL

THERE ARE 200 THINGS YOU CAN BE DOING EVERY DAY to sell your product and, in the process, build your brand. With so many possibilities, the problem arises of where to begin. The resultant brain freeze can result in a paralysis and, instead of accomplishing a tenth of those options, you sit staring idly at your computer screen. It's the terror of the blank page.

PILLAR ONE: GENERATE IDEAS

"Distraction is doom! Money flows to rapid results; drifting execution gets impoverished."

— JIM TREACY, FORMER PRESIDENT/
COO, MONSTER WORLDWIDE

I subscribe to an idea that I heard from James Altucher about generating ideas. He said that he tries every day to come up with 10 ideas. Now, if you come up with 10 great ideas on behalf of your brand, that's terrific. But the point of this exercise—and it is an exercise—is to flex that idea-generating muscle. As with any muscle, you must use it or lose it. And the more you use it, the stronger it gets.

Your most valuable asset is your earning ability and, like a new car that is driven off the lot, it is depreciating as soon as you graduate college. Of course, there are things you can do to that vehicle to raise its value: install a state-of-the-art stereo, replace the standard rims with high-end rims, get a custom paint job, and so on. Likewise, unless you are making upgrades in your own life by learning and generating new ideas, you are depreciating in value.

If you're adding either skills or ideas as part of your daily routine, you are flipping the script, appreciating your value rather than decreasing it. There's a synergy that happens as well because if you are attempting to differentiate yourself by adding appreciation to your worth, you are more likely to arrive at new ideas. If you're reading business books and listening to audiobooks in the car, attending conferences and feeding your head with the wisdom of successful leaders, you will necessarily trigger new ideas from that input.

You will notice that throughout this book, I am referencing the ideas of others—sharing the ideas that I've learned from them and incorporating their suggestions into my own plan of action. There are people who have inspired me and I enjoy giving them attribution for their contribution.

I have a portion of my blog that I devote to the notion of success, and I interview people who have attained it so that my readers can benefit from their knowledge. I know enough to know that I am not going to come up with all the answers. That is why I expose myself to people much smarter than I am. And by doing so, I am getting different ideas and new ways that I can apply them in my life.

I even turned those interviews into an eBook titled Just Like You: 24 Interviews of Ordinary People Who've Achieved Extraordinary Success.

For example, my very first blog post was about the fatal flaw of paying for performance. I wrote it because I worked at an ad network and it was purely a performance-based cost-per-acquisition version of that (don't worry, this won't be on the test). If an advertiser like Blockbuster wanted to put an ad on our ad network for a new subscription model client, we would put it on our ad network—a closed publisher network, meaning that the advertiser did not know where the ad was going to run. The publishers would take that banner ad, put it on their website, and if somebody registered for Blockbuster on their website, then that affiliate would get paid a certain percentage for it and the ad network would get a certain percentage, and the advertiser gets a new client.

The reason I addressed this concept in my blog was because I had read a *Harvard Business Review* article about the slippery slope of how some CEOs get into trouble for cooking the books, and this article indicated that CEOs were receiving incentives for the wrong reasons, such as stock performance, which would get them into trouble because it enticed them to cook the books in an attempt to make it appear that the stock was over-performing.

I addressed the issue and then I mapped it to what I did in my life; applied the idea, that is, to my own work environment. I gave credit to the *Harvard Business Review*, saying, "I just read an article about the fatal flaw of paper performance for these CEOs. Here is how it applies to my industry."

By doing so, I was now coming at the matter from a completely different angle than most people had probably ever conceived of it. By providing additional ideas and feedback and pro-actively offering thoughts and processes to your prospects, your boss, and your internal organization, you are potentially changing the way things work.

In this particular case, the fatal flaw in the ad network was that when the publisher was being paid by the conversion, the risk was that he would naturally feel an incentive to use black-hat techniques to get that conversion. What I mean by that is the publisher might be inclined to dupe a person into giving them their credit card information, saying, "Sign up for a free subscription to Blockbuster, but we still need your credit card information." And then, seven days later, they might come back and say that it's now a monthly subscription. That's where things really get ugly. And that's the fatal flaw of paying for performance.

By exposing yourself to different ideas outside your industry, you will stimulate your own ideas. Once you start exposing yourself to smarter people and trying to apply it to your industry and what you're doing, you will become better at it.

You might, for instance, hear a principle that you can apply interdisciplinarily, like Occam's Razor. Suppose you hear a podcast or read something in a book about the tenet (simply put, "all else being equal, the simpler explanation is the better one") and realize how it applies to your own line of work. That wisdom you acquired you can now put in applicable terms and you can dispense to your audience.

When I meet with people, I try to offer them 10 ideas. Being on TV has given me access to a lot of people whom I otherwise might not have met. The Green Room is a networking hub where I often encounter people of different walks of life. While waiting to go on camera not long ago, I encountered some executives from the New York City Ballet. They asked me what it was that I did for a living and I explained that I owned a digital marketing company. They explained that they and their dancers used social media quite a bit.

"Do you leverage social media to sell tickets?" I asked. They did not. The ball was now rolling. I threw out some ideas—ideas that I was able to generate on the spot because I spend each day practicing it.

They were excused from the room to prepare for their segment. They were gone five minutes. In that time, I had jotted down 10 ideas. I gave them the list when they sat back down. I told them that these ideas would help them leverage their social media.

Now, I didn't close a deal from that. I don't know whether I will ever close a deal from that, but I know that if I don't make that effort, I certainly won't. I start from the point of always wanting to give and add value. If that ever boomerangs back and I end up closing the deal as a result, it is only because I'm adding value.

The fact is, it is easier to generate ideas if you are following your passion. I am passionate about digital and social media, so naturally, I think about it all the time. When I considered the New York City Ballet and rambled off those 10 ideas—I use the word "rambled" because it took me about three minutes to conceive of those ideas and maybe it took me five minutes to write it out longhand because I rarely write anything out longhand and I wanted to make it legible for them—I was moving the ball down the field. It's a wonderful way to begin a business relationship. And that can be done in the real world or the virtual one.

By offering these ideas, I am differentiating myself from my competitors. I am providing an added value that goes above and beyond the expectations that have been placed on me.

It seems very daunting but, if you work out, just remember how daunting the weight you're now lifting or the miles you're now running seemed when you first began. Start small and work your way up. Give yourself the freedom to think outside the box (and I'm aware of how "in the box" that phrase is). Ask yourself what you would do for your business if money were no object or if you were not tied down to a specific location. It is too easy to get myopic in your vision and stuck in a rut if you are not willing to explore the seemingly impossible.

Once you are generating new and creative ideas, you need to share those. And that brings us back to the ever-important blog. Blog, blog, blog, and blog some more. If you haven't already done so, go to LinkedIn, upload an image, write your content, add a couple of tags, post it, and it will automatically make its way to the people whom you're connected to on the network.

"My blog changed my career trajectory," venture capitalist Tim Flannery told me. "It opened more doors than I imagined. Social media has just changed how I experience events," he said. "My devices and all its apps and software have become a passive extension of me."

If you write really good content, people will start to follow you. Now, all of a sudden, a community of people are listening. And as Chris Guerrero, a CrossFit affiliate owner and trainer, says, "Community, above all else, drives product." And now you are already 10 steps ahead of the game. You don't have to try to find that audience. You don't have to curate the audience. By virtue of your network and the vertical you work in, you have people who will pay attention to the content that you are writing about.

If you're concerned because you don't feel that your content is appropriate for LinkedIn, use Medium.com, which is super simple and beautiful. It is easy to generate content and similar to LinkedIn in that the cream rises to the top. If you generate good material and you post it here, then tweet it out and put it on your Facebook page, you will gain a following of readers. It really is that easy to get started.

If you feel a little bit more advanced and you really want to go start to curate your own content, start a WordPress blog. WordPress allows you to expeditiously create a URL with your first and last name, and it will allow you to have branding equity based on that. You don't necessarily need to name the blog immediately. Just use your first and last name and you can blog about any old thing you want—even *Star Wars* or Smurfs.

WordPress is also helpful because it allows you to upload themes. This is where a little bit of money finally comes in handy. And not a lot of money. The theme that I uploaded for my Silverback Social (as well as the Westchester Digital Summit and christopherdessi.com) cost me just $75 and every time that the theme updates, I just hit an automatic update option. It happens to be a powerful theme with search engine optimization tools on it. It is also super intuitive to navigate—you can navigate a Word document or a PowerPoint document or an Excel document.

If, on the other hand, you are a visually inclined person and you are generating photography content, let's say, and you don't want to deal with the written word, then leverage Tumblr and start a blog on it with just images. Humans of New York was started on a Tumblr and included just photographs of people in New York whose answers to a couple of profound questions were posted, sort of like a digital coffee table book. It was really beautiful.

If you don't even want to blog but you just want to be inspired and create your own vision boards, start a Pinterest board and leverage it. Curate your own content so that when people Google you, they find your content on it and learn more about you. It is yet another way to connect and it doesn't require any writing on your part. It also doesn't require any real creativity on your part. But by sharing your interests with others, you have helped break the ice, making any potential encounter much smoother.

If, however, you do want to write but what is stopping you is the quality of your writing, there are fixes for that, too. Maybe you're like I am—I'm an idea man. I get tons of ideas. I jot them down all over the place and over the years, they've added up. I have so many ideas, in fact, that this book was born out of them.

But I'm not William Faulkner. I know that. I have editors who clean up my writing and make it flow better. If you are blogging and you feel confident enough to get your content read, use the Hemingway app like I do, which, as I mentioned earlier, lets you know the grade level of your writing so that you can be more effective. You want to be able to explain things to a six-year-old. James Altucher is a master at this. He writes in very simple language that sounds as if he is speaking. It is probably written at a fourth- or fifth-grade level. To put that in some context, Ernest Hemingway's *The Old Man and the Sea*, a compelling work of literature, was written at a fourth-grade level.

The Wall Street Journal is written at maybe a seventh-grade level and is considered a very highbrow publication. You don't want your material to be written at a 12th-grade level despite the fact that, as communications majors, some of us have been taught to write that way. Lose that habit. Remember William of Occam: simpler is better.

There are, of course, many other apps to leverage, but one of my favorites, which I mentioned earlier, is CoSchedule. Like a virtual assistant, once you create your content, this app will not only publish it but will analyze your best-performing pieces of content. It will then repost your solidly performing content at later dates. This is very important because as you generate content, you will eventually have a repository of old material. But that material may still be quite relevant and by getting it back out to the world, you are essentially getting compound interest.

The first time you posted a particular article, your whole eco-system of friends, family, and colleagues might not have seen it. But if you post it a second and a third time, they might find it. There is a calendar in the app that makes it very simple to post the content and to spread it out. This is called scaling. When you have the ability to scale by leveraging simple technologies, it becomes a hugely compelling and valuable tool for your blog. Regenerating your content this way is like getting work done while you sleep.

I have reposted content that I created two years earlier because it became relevant again. I will post it on Twitter sometimes and say, "Here's an oldie but a goodie."

So when I say you can do 200 things to help your brand every single day, I'm underestimating. There are probably two million things you could be doing.

PILLAR TWO: DEFINE YOUR PASSION

"All truly successful people I know have passion. To be truly successful at something, you have to love it."

— RUSS ADLER, OWNER, LAW OFFICES
OF RUSSELL E. ADLER, PLCC

I listened to mega-influencer Gary Vaynerchuk speak at the Web 2.0 Conference. He really impressed me. I wrote him a page-long impassioned email asking him to meet with me, saying that the way he explained it, social media sounded like the greatest thing since sliced bread.

I went to New Jersey to meet him and told him I was excited about social media and wanted to work with him. As I mentioned earlier, he pointed out that I had a wife, a child, and a mortgage back on my home in Chappaqua. He said he couldn't afford me, that he was paying young people straight out of college $22,000 a year, and that there was no way he was going to hire someone making six figures. Instead, he gave me some advice.

"What are you passionate about?" he asked me. I told him that I was really passionate about business. "Go deeper," he told me. I thought about it for a moment and concluded that I was really passionate about being a father. "Great," he said, "Take that and go do social media."

I went home and thought about my homework assignment. I did some research and discovered there were already a bunch of dad blogs out there. To expound upon what I touched on earlier, I bought a URL called Dadzilla.com because that was a hook: I wasn't just a dad, I was a dadzilla. I put up a digital camera in my home, did my best Gary Vaynerchuk impression, and began doing video reviews. I began:

"Hello, everybody. My name is Chris Dessi. Welcome to Dadzilla TV. Dadzilla TV is going to be a place where we review products for children. We're going to talk about being a great dad. What it takes to be a great dad."

Before the awful truth about the family came out, I remember saying, "I'm going to talk about *Jon & Kate Plus 8*. They've got eight kids and he's a super dad. He's an ultimate dad." (Again, this was before Jon's scandalous behavior surfaced.) "I can't

wait," I told my audience, "to talk to you about being a father."
Boom. It was only about 30 seconds long, but there it was,
posted on Dadzilla TV.

I was pretty active on Twitter at that point, so I tweeted the
content. I gave it a couple of hashtags (#fatherhood, #dad)
and the next thing I knew, a man in the neighboring town
of Pleasantville found it and retweeted it, saying something
like, "Hey, social media people in Westchester. Check out this
impassioned video from this local resident. It says in his profile he's from Chappaqua. Isn't this really exciting?"

All of a sudden—and I'm telling you, this didn't take months;
this didn't take weeks; this was days later—I had a whole
ecosystem of people who were interested in the content I was
generating. I was in awe that this stuff really worked. I was
blown away by it. I kept studying what Gary was doing, and
he kept saying, "You define what you're passionate about, you
start generating the content."

I started generating the content by just doing reviews. I had a
flip cam, back when they were popular, and I started talking
about being a dad and how convenient it was to have a flip
cam. I said, "It's great having a flip cam because I'm push-
ing the stroller down the street and I see my daughter doing
something really cute, and I just hop on the flip cam and take
a video of her. It's really compelling."

I remember I posted it on Facebook and my friends thought
that I was now selling flip cams. I explained that I was just
doing a review.

A couple of weeks later, Gary did a video on his Wine Library site and said, "People keep asking me how to monetize yourself in social media. I'm going to show you." He picked up the phone, called somebody, and said, "I have a blog about wine. Would you be interested in sponsoring it?"

The person on the other end of the phone asked how many viewers Gary had. "I get 30,000 viewers per night," he replied. The other guy was "absolutely interested" in sponsoring it.

"That's how you monetize it," Gary said, looking directly into the camera.

He literally videotaped himself cold calling somebody to try to monetize the content that he was generating. It gave me ideas (remember Pillar One? Be generating ideas). For starters, I found the guy who did the intro to Wine Library, which was something of a visual introduction with a guitar riff. I emailed him and asked how much he would charge to do something similar for my Dadzilla TV. He did it for about $200.

I also decided to reach out to the authors of some books about fatherhood, which I had been given as gifts, being a new father. I found some of the people on Twitter and on their websites, and I would just email them and ask, "Would you like to collaborate on a book?" I had one guy say, "Yeah, I'd love to write a book with you. I saw your content. It's great." I ended up taking a new job, however, and had to phase out the Dadzilla stuff.

The point is, figure out what you're passionate about and

that will help you get started. I talked to TV journalist Chris Hansen about passion. And he believes it is the key to success. "You need to like and believe in what you are doing," Hansen said. "You also have to convince others to support you and believe in you."

If you're looking for passion, Chris Guerrero is a fountain of it. He told me that he's never been motivated by money, and if you know the guy, you know he's being honest. "I'm motivated by enjoying what I do," he told me, "and sharing my passion for fitness with others." That kind of passion is contagious.

Remember, too, that a passion is more than just what you like to do. Everybody I know likes to shop. Who doesn't like to get nice things? But is there any skill involved in that? Maybe there is if you have a certain talent. I have a friend who is a very successful jewelry designer in Las Vegas. When she shows me her jewelry pieces, I realize that she is functioning at a different level than other people. The reason why is that she has a degree in jewelry design and has put in the hours.

Blogging about jewelry is probably difficult—you need to actually see the jewelry, not just read about it. There are visual-based platforms, such as Pinterest, Tumblr, Instagram, and the like, where you can create pin-up boards to articulate what inspires you in ways that words cannot.

Based on what your business is and where you want to take it, there are platforms that will help you start building your personal brand. If you're sitting on the beach, uncertain of what you're passionate about but decide "I just like the beach," great. You've identified your passion. Now, start visiting more beaches and review them for others, write about what you like and don't like about particular beaches, get a following of similarly minded people, and then approach a travel company and see if they're willing to sponsor a trip or provide you with resources. Talk to beachwear companies about their brands.

Chances are, it will take time before you gain the level of expertise necessary to be a thought leader in your field or develop enough of a following to be an influencer. But no one ever said that building your brand was not without work.

I have had young people, straight out of college, ask me how they can get invited to be a keynote speaker. I point out that you have to actually do something before people want to pay you to talk about something. I explain that I started out at a local Chamber of Commerce in 2008 because I wanted to be a thought leader within my organization. I gave the speech for free. I drove two hours out to Long Island—the middle of nowhere, Long Island—and I was just horrible.

That experience turned out to be great, however, because I was then able to put "speaker" on my résumé as a result. Now I could work at honing that craft and continue working on it and put in my 10,000 hours (that amount of practice necessary to master something, per Malcolm Gladwell).

Find what it is you love to do and get proficient at it. Success dwells at the fulcrum of passion and excellence. I'm passionate about a lot of things that I know I'm not so amazing at and that I definitely can't make a living at. I love playing guitar.

My daughter loves when I play songs from the movie *Frozen*. It's fun. I'm never going to be a rock star. I'm certainly not dedicating 10,000 hours to it.

PILLAR THREE: WORK, FOCUS, AND PERSIST

"It is called hard work because it's hard. It's not easy to be in business for yourself or in any business. It's not the lucky who win, but the relentless that succeed in the end."

— JEFF HAYZLETT, FORMER CHIEF
MARKETING OFFICER, EASTMAN KODAK

There is an anecdote I've heard about Warren Buffett, Bill Gates, and Gates' father at a dinner party. A guest asked them what the most important quality for success was today and all three responded "focus" at the same exact time. They all smiled and laughed to each other because they hadn't really prepared the answer. And the irony of them all chiming in simultaneously is that, as they attested, today's world is filled with a barrage of distraction that comes at us from all angles.

Social media is part of that cacophony. We are inundated with tweets and texts and emails that are no longer just work interruptions, but because of the mini-computers we carry around in our pockets, this flood of information distracts us wherever we happen to be, 24/7.

It becomes critical, if you're looking to be successful, to define what it is you want to accomplish. I find this is tremendously helpful in my own life. Write down your goals in any form that works best for you—on a whiteboard, in the notes section of your iPhone or, like I do, by literally putting pen to paper. It doesn't matter. Just be as specific as you possibly can.

If your passion is to be a fashion blogger, go deeper with it: "I want to draw 10,000 views per day to my online space and generate $2,000 a month in revenues." And so on. Shoot for laser precision rather than shotgun spread. When you get specific like that, good things happen because when you combine that focus with a passion and skill, success follows. As I said earlier, success dwells at the fulcrum of passion and excellence.

There is a trick that firemen use to break car windshields when they need to get inside. With just their hands, they are able to break a windshield by tapping along with a lot of pressure. They tap consistently: tap, tap, tap, tap, tap, tap and soon, the whole pane of glass shatters. You can't shatter a windshield with a sledgehammer if you strike in the wrong spot because they are exceptionally well-built. The firemen use this trick, which is all about locating their focal point and aggressively chipping away at it persistently.

Bill LaRosa, a business/personal growth consultant and angel investor, says that along with flexibility, the other trait that he developed early on which helped him most in his career is persistence.

Real estate wiz Raymond Sanseverino is of the same mind. He once told me that his recipe for success is "determination coupled with a willingness to work hard." He said he doesn't know anyone who is successful who does not work hard.

There are a few layers that are necessary to keep yourself from distraction. You need to surround yourself with people who are going to support you and your vision. For example, my business partner, John Zanzarella, was a helpful support structure for me when my father was going through the final stages of his battle with Lou Gehrig's disease. I was distracted both emotionally and physically by frequent hospital visits, helping my mother through it, and, along with my brother, handling my father's estate. I also had to deal with insurance issues. And all the while, I still had a wife and children at home.

And I understand someone always has it worse. But we all face seemingly insurmountable obstacles in our lives and the only way to get through situations like that with your health and sanity intact is by staying focused and leaning on the people in your life who share your vision and are able to help you deal with the stress.

What I learned going through that ordeal with my dying father was that meditation combined with physical activity and a healthy lifestyle was the only way that I was able to survive it. Having a support system in place made it possible for me to keep moving forward. My business partner would often say, "Chris, go inside and meditate." He would see the look on my face and understand that I needed 20 minutes.

I would go into the conference room, meditate, and give myself breathing room. I would pay attention to my breaths and to where my head was at. Then, I'd be able to recharge that battery. Not only did this do wonders for my focus, but by developing a routine, I had to be persistent. Nothing has furthered my career more than that trait: persistence.

9 Simple Ways to Motivate Yourself Every Day

There are myriad psychology models and theories on what motivates us to do the things we do—how we respond to incentives, achievement theories, and so on. I look at motivation as excitement. So how can you remain motivated in a simple way that works every single day?

1. Take a Break. You Deserve it.

The only way we can perform at an optimal level is to create time for rest. The moment you know you can't take any time off is usually when you need it most. So take that long delayed vacation and return to your business with renewed enthusiasm.

2. Keep Your Cards Close to Your Chest.

Finally running that marathon? Excited about your new diet? Bursting at the seams over your new project? Good. Keep it to yourself. Announcing your intent to do these feats will backfire. Resist the urge to reap the barrage of Facebook "likes" and gushing comments. The positive feedback you receive from you network will trick your brain into thinking you've already accomplished your goal, sabotaging your once motivated brain to do said feat. So keep it to yourself and share the good news once you've already done it.

3. Confront Death and Define Your Legacy

Death is a powerful motivator. We get bogged down in mindless activities. They make us feel like we're accomplishing things, when in reality we're just spinning in circles. Knowing that you have finite time on this planet helps to sharpen your focus. Everything we do is another step in defining our legacy. This may seem like heady posturing, but both can be powerful motivators.

4. Celebrate the Little Wins, No Matter How Small

Little wins may seem like just that: little. But celebrating these wins can help to create positive habits. You break the inertia of mediocrity by teaching everyone around you how to win. They get the chance to bask in that emotion. Vishen Lakhiani, CEO of Mindvalley, has gone so far as implementing what he calls the "Awesome Bell," which he rings (you guessed it) any time something awesome happens.

5. Slash Your To-Do List in Half

Slashing your aggressive to-do list in half will allow room

for success. Knowing that it's realistic for you to complete the list is empowering.

6. Be Gentle with Yourself

Stop comparing the accomplishments in your life with those of your neighbor. The story you create in your head will never be as good and the reality will never be as bad. There are many people who are smarter than you. The moment you can embrace this notion, you're free: free to explore; free to follow what excites you; free to ignore what they do, or how they do it, and focus on you.

7. Hack the Way Your Brain Perceives Your New Habits

Recently I began waking up two hours earlier than usual during the week. Instead of viewing it as two hours less I get to sleep, I view it as two extra hours to my day, allowing me to add a full workday per week.

8. Embrace Vulnerability

We live in a culture where we horde Instagram followers and Facebook "likes." The perception of our lives being anything less than perfect is a daunting notion. The glossy Facebookification of our lives can create a dangerous façade of success. Sharing defeats and admitting failure is a powerful cultivator of motivation, allowing you to move past the failure. Work through the emotion instead of taking it out on someone else. Then move on to something more constructive. Sharing these vulnerable moments also cultivates deeper connection with peers.

9. Do What You Love (Sort Of)

Like I said earlier, find what it is you love to do and get proficient at it. Success dwells at the fulcrum of passion and excellence, but only if you can make a living from your passion. I'm passionate about a lot of things that I know I'm not so amazing at and that I definitely can't make a living at. I love playing guitar, but I'm never going to be a rock star.

Other times, John would say, "Chris, go exercise. Go do Cross-Fit." I would carve out time for myself to exercise. I'm not suggesting that everybody needs an hour out of their day to work out but if you need a break, take a walk around the block. You need to give your body a chance to catch up to your racing mind. The only way that you're going to be able to do that is to wrangle your frantic mind and separate your body so you can tap into all the things that can come from defining what you're passionate about.

Meditation is a skill that needs to be honed through practice. It is not an easy thing. Close your eyes and breathe in through your nose and out through your mouth for 10 solid minutes without thinking a single thought. It's near impossible. Our brains, in this very hectic world in which we live, are programmed to be thinking about a billion other things. I've got to pick up the kids, get to the gym, pick up the dry-cleaning, did I leave the stove on?

This digression is the source of counter-productivity and can lead to depression. The first step in the right direction is to find a quiet space where you are able to have a moment to yourself. While I was dealing with my father's declining illness, that space was in the midst of raising two beautiful daughters and running a thriving digital agency. I was also in the midst of developing and launching a nationally-recognized annual event and making national television appearances. Meditation and exercise were my tools to avoid a nervous breakdown.

In the final days of my father's life, I was sleeping in my parents' basement and my whole family was around. Aunts and uncles flew in because we knew that he was in declining health. Every day, I would extricate myself and go downstairs to meditate for 20 minutes using an app called Headspace. I highly recommend it for beginners because it gives you something called guided meditation, which allows you to just listen and follow directions.

When I was down in the basement, I would finish the meditation and start my workout. I would do at-home workouts that were similar to CrossFit movements: push-ups, jumping jacks, stretching, and other similar exercises—anything that would get my blood flowing, my heart rate up, and allow me to tap into something healthful. It allowed for me to get about a 45-minute respite from what was happening upstairs and being confronted with the idea that I was losing my father. It was literally the only thing, I believe, that sustained my mental, emotional, and physical stability, keeping me from dropping dead, myself, of a heart attack.

Focus also involves considering the people with whom you spend your time. For instance, how do you decide who to meet and for what purposes? This is a tough one for me as I struggle with the time involved in meeting people. But I have had fortuitous meetings because I was willing to take the time. In the years that I've been running my own company, I've become much better at determining the people with whom I spend my time by gauging the types of questions they ask me.

If somebody is coming to me with an opportunity, let's say, they can usually identify what that is pretty quickly. However, if they just want to rub elbows with me and pick my brain, I can generally determine that pretty fast. Those requests usually begin, "Can I take you to dinner?" When they're offering to pay for something, that's usually a red flag for me. If a person has something to talk about, I will just hop on a call and discuss it. The ability to determine whether a meeting is a waste of time or not is something that, frankly, I'm still learning.

Being able to choose how you spend that time is very important. The one thing that I've been able to figure out in order to remain focused is that I now no longer schedule meetings before 3:00 p.m. This is a recently-implemented rule. The afternoon hours between 3:00 p.m. and 5:00 p.m. I have found to be the best portion of the day for me to take phone calls and meetings. Because my business moves so quickly and is driven in large part by real-time content, mornings are very difficult times for me to remove myself for a phone call or a breakfast meeting or a coffee. If that's something that will help you, use it. Block out that time and only take calls between those two hours at the end of the day. Schedule for no more than 20-30 minutes each. Your time will be much more productive.

PILLAR FOUR: BECOME MORE SELF-AWARE

"A trait I see among successful people is not worrying about what other people think of you. Be yourself and don't be afraid to speak your mind and try different things."
— DENNIS SIMMONS, CEO, WASC HOLDING, LLC

As I've said, I'm an idea man. I can be an inspiring and motivating communicator in front of a crowd or a camera. I'm good at these things. I also understand what I am not so good at. I am horrible—borderline learning disability—with mathematics.

I once took a battery of tests that examined the stress levels of military operatives. I was hooked up to machines that monitored my body temperature and pulse as I answered questions. Keep in mind that I can barely—and this the God's honest truth—figure out the tip in a restaurant. I hand it to my wife, who is a fifth-grade math teacher and does the math in our home. And let me point out that I scored a perfect score on my SATs in the verbal section. I just stink at math. So when the results of that battery of tests were calculated, the guy who administered the tests said, "It's almost like there was brain damage here." He literally used the words "brain damage."

So what do I do to compensate for my math deficiency? I surround myself with people who have that skill and I don't pretend that I am one of them. Before I created the Westchester Digital Summit, I had never done an event before. Back then, I was doing business with a law firm that invited me to an event that involved a golf outing at Pinehurst, and while I was there, the man who was running the event was actually in my foursome (the man would later become my business partner, John Zanzarella).

"How are you out here playing golf with us?" I asked. "Aren't you supposed to be running the event?" John explained that he ran events annually and knew how to manage things to the point where the event would practically run itself. "It's all good," he said. "Don't worry."

Now, this was an event that had about 200 lawyers in attendance. I'm talking about type-A people who pay extremely careful attention to detail. And John, to his credit, is satisfying their level of scrutiny at a ridiculously high level and simultaneously playing golf with me. So a couple of months later, when I begin to plan an event around a URL that I've purchased, WestchesterDigitalSummit.com, I feel the confidence that I might be able to do this.

I realized I could get speakers and that I could be on stage as the master of ceremonies. I could call up Gary Vaynerchuk to keynote the event and get people from Facebook and LinkedIn as well as a Fox News anchor and my friend Jeff Pearlman, a *New York Times* bestselling author. What I knew I couldn't do was keep the books because I have no idea how to do that. I certainly didn't know how to book an event or manage one. So I called up John, who told me that his parents had been doing event marketing in Westchester for the past 25 years and that we should meet. Within five minutes of meeting his father, we shook hands and created a 50/50 partnership for the Westchester Digital Summit.

Understanding your weaknesses is the best place to start for success. People who don't understand their weaknesses get into trouble. People who try to pretend their way through things and work on the façade of having the knowledge are setting themselves up for failure. This is a major downfall for social media, as people who have not yet put in their 10,000 hours can suddenly find themselves in a position of leadership or authority based on their following, and without understanding their limitations, they often dispense really bad advice and flop as a result.

Of course, the flip side of this is that the true experts, the ones who supply really good advice, eventually rise to the top.

I don't want you, after reading this book, to be a flop. You need to be able to understand what it is that you're good at. If you can get in front of a camera and you can talk until you turn blue in the face, then get in front of a camera. If you can write, then write. If you can't write, find someone who can do that part of the job for you. If you can't pull off an event, find people who can. Understand your weaknesses and blind spots and surround yourself with people who can help you in the areas of your life where you're least proficient.

PILLAR FIVE: DO GOOD, GIVE BACK

"I'm a huge believer in gratitude. I handwrite three thank you cards each morning and spend each dinner with my family, going around the table, all sharing someone we're grateful for that day. Gratitude is the best drug on the planet."
— DAVE KERPEN, FOUNDER/CEO, LIKEABLE LOCAL

Giving back to others has birthed so much good in both my personal and career life. I started small, really small. One pivotal occurrence was my wedding anniversary in 2009. I just began listing things on my blog that I was grateful for. I would just sit down and think of maybe five things in my life for which I felt blessed.

Among the things I listed, this being around the time of my anniversary, was my wife. I wrote a blog post about how I fell in love with her and how much I adored her. I was just trying to express to her how important she really was in my life.

I had enjoyed a healthy bachelorhood. You might say I was aggressively single. I lived in Manhattan and was having a blast. And being single in London was wild. But I came back and started dating the woman who would become my wife—a woman whom I had met for the first time when I was five-years-old. We were reintroduced and set up by my mother when I was 29. And the only way I can articulate the experience of being with her was that it reintroduced me to who I really was. She reintroduced me to that five-year-old kid because when I was with her I felt like the real me rather than some studly bachelor who had to put on airs and take a girl out to a ridiculously fancy restaurant.

For putting me back in touch with myself, I was and am forever grateful to her. And when I articulated that in a blog post, it received a really incredible reaction.

So, not long after that and still riding high from the reaction, I decided to write handwritten notes to everybody who was going to be at dinner at my home for Thanksgiving. The response was really overwhelming. I passed out handwritten notes to everybody sitting at the dining room table. I stood up and gave a toast, saying, "You can read your note now or you can read it later, but these are the reasons why I am grateful that you are in my life."

It opened up a spot in my heart and in everybody else's heart that day at Thanksgiving and I realized that simply telling people how much you love and value them is really compelling.

John Dokes, whom I've quoted earlier, told me that he tries to create happiness and leave a positive legacy, saying that we all have a potential that can be either "extended or diminished depending on the paths we choose." Each day, he actively tries to make things better on his path.

There was a very popular book you might recall titled *The Secret*, which I really liked and it changed my thinking about things. The idea of just deciding to be in a good mood was transformative for me. I understood that I could simply change my approach to certain matters just by giving myself permission to. It is what led me to meditation and was instrumental in the success I've attained in my life. I draw inspiration from it.

While I was working as a sales executive at Buddy Media, I sat across from an intern. The young man's name was Andrew Gothelf and because no one could pronounce his last name, we called him "Gotti"—not because he had any resemblance to anyone in the mafia family but because his last name was pretty close to that. He was a nice, Jewish kid from Maryland studying journalism at Northwestern.

I really took a shine to the young man. He was super smart, very humble, asked a lot of really good questions, and was willing to learn. He was really open to everything that was happening in the company.

He knew how passionate I was about social media and would read my blog posts. He wanted to learn more about blogging. I was shocked that a journalism student was not already blogging.

He asked me why he needed a blog and I told him, "If you're a junior in college and you write a blog post once a week, you will have a portfolio by the time you graduate, which you can send to any major newspaper in the country and say, 'Yeah, I've been writing for the past two years. Look at how great my writing is.' Otherwise, you're going to have to manually put that into a résumé and try to articulate what a great writer you are on a résumé. Start blogging."

That conversation was on a Friday. By Monday, he had not only figured out how to create a WordPress blog, but he was also on his fifth blog post. He was getting comments on it from his friends and family because he was writing about sports broadcasting, which he wanted to pursue. Immediately, he had a following.

I wrote a blog post of my own. At the time, there was a reality TV show called *Growing Up Gotti*, which featured John Gotti, the legendary gangster's grandson. I called the blog post "Growing up Gotti" because I knew it would get some traction. In it, I just sung the accolades of this young man who sat across from me because he had figured it out. He had shown humility, listened, and executed. I thought that was one of the most pure examples of conversation to conception to idea to execution to processes ever.

People went nuts over the post, telling me that it was really incredible. The kid eventually ended up working at Buddy Media after he graduated and later went on to an amazing career at social media software companies. By virtue of singing the praises of others I admire, I have developed and strengthened relationships.

Today, Gotti is a colleague of mine. He attended the most recent Westchester Digital Summit. I get to hug this guy who is now a thriving executive in my world and it was all because of a mere conversation about writing a blog.

I have since written blog posts about those other inspiring people in my life, singing their praises publicly. When I see people doing really good things, which light a fire under me to do good things in the world, I like patting them on the back in as broad and as bombastic a manner as I possibly can. It just brings joy to me. That has migrated into the "Success Feature" on my blog that I mentioned earlier, where I get to find people who really inspire me, ask them 10 or 15 compelling questions, and share with the world all the great work that they're doing.

When you start talking positively about people who are doing things that inspire you, those words attract other positive-minded people who are interested in improving themselves, who are interested in taking their lives to a different level and improving their game. And then, those people are drawn to you and you find yourself surrounded by like-minded people. That's not just sitting on the sidelines, watching life pass you by. On the contrary, that is living.

"Just be a good person," former Marine Chris Maloney told me. "Stand up for what is right. If you care enough about something or somebody, you'll find the right opportunity and make luck happen. If it doesn't happen, take a breath—maybe a Jameson—and try harder. Put the left in front of the right, keep moving, and occasionally give high fives to people you don't know. Enjoy it all and don't stop believing."

That's some solid advice from a solid human being.

PILLAR SIX: USE TECHNOLOGY THE RIGHT WAY

"I try to keep up with the explosive changes in all media, especially digital. Whether it's my Kickstarter campaign or doing a Reddit AMA to promote a new show, you have to stay on top of all this. I do it by surrounding myself with young, smart people."

— CHRIS HANSEN, TV JOURNALIST, AUTHOR

When I encourage people to create their personal digital brand identities, it is because it is the most efficient way of reaching the most amount of people. I'm not suggesting that it should replace in-person networking, face to face meetings, or doing good offline. But by leveraging this technology, it is possible to supplement and add value to the in-person networking that you do.

I recall going to conferences where I saw elements that I didn't like, which used to get me upset as being a waste of time. I would fly out to San Diego for a conference and would see everything there was to see in the first five minutes. And so then, I have to pay for the hotel and go out and network with the same knuckleheads who are at the rest of the conferences.

So here is where technology comes in. For $7.99, I bought WestchesterDigitalSummit.com from godaddy.com and created my own event out of thin air. It was literally that simple. I bought the URL, posted the website, got somebody to create a logo, and announced, "We've got an event."

I found the right partners, networked with those people, and said, "Let's figure this out." I started calling friends that I knew would be right for the event. I started creating my dream event based on the things that I would want to learn if I were attending. I figured out what the audience would potentially be interested in and developed the conference around that. By just leveraging the technology, I shifted my position from being under-the-thumb as an attendee to being the curator of the event and the master of ceremonies.

That is a huge leap. I went from stroking checks to attend an event to being the event organizer and having the checks land in my pocket. Why? Simply because I came up with an idea, focused on what it was that I wanted to accomplish, and understood what I was passionate about and good at. I tapped into my network of people I admired to get other speakers to celebrate their knowledge. From every angle, it was the most complete and efficient win-win-win-win situation. And it all began with my conceiving of the idea of leveraging technologies.

And you can do it, too. You can go on LinkedIn right now and create a group. Maybe you sell fake brick fixtures (I'm looking at a brick wall in my office and finding inspiration). You title your group "Fake Brick Fixture Sales Guy Networking Group" or something maybe a little less on-the-nose than that. You can search on LinkedIn and find every fake brick fixture salesperson on the site. You can then go on Twitter, find all those guys, and invite them to your group. You came up with an idea, figured out what you were passionate about and good at, and you are now the curator of an online community.

Or you could just wait behind the velvet rope for someone to invite you into their group. And you can complain that it isn't run the way you would run it. Would you rather wait in line to go to a restaurant or own your own restaurant? By leveraging technology, you have the opportunity to be the restaurateur rather than the patron.

Technology is a great equalizer. You might be painfully shy around people but by using the technology of social media, you can interact with others in a way that you might never have thought possible. And when you do attend in-person conferences or events, there are technologies that can mitigate that social awkwardness as well. Lanyard.com, for instance, is a site that allows you to sync your social media contacts with the attendees of events you will be attending. That way, you know who to expect and can prepare appropriately.

This also allows you to network with attendees whom you are interested in talking with. You can start to establish a business relationship with someone before you ever even step foot off the plane.

PILLAR SEVEN: GET CURIOUS

"If I decide today I want to get into a book, I'll start today and I won't stop, and I'll read two to three books a week."
— ADRIAN DESSI, BUSINESSMAN, HUSBAND, FATHER

Ask questions of people who have succeeded before you. You

need to be the person who asks the right questions at the right time through the right people. If you are not asking questions, you are going to fail. If you don't understand where the chinks in your armor are, you are going to fail.

Suppose you are looking for a job. Where do you start? How is getting curious going to help you land a job? Begin by proactively reaching out to the most powerful people in your network. Actually start from the top and work your way down. Say, "I would like to meet you for an informational interview." Even consider going so far as saying, "I would like to have a consulting meeting with you and I am going to pay you $200 for an hour of your time." I dare you.

Find the most powerful person that you can and offer to pay them. I'm willing to bet you they'll say, "Don't worry about the money. Let's meet. You must have a lot of really burning questions on your plate." Show up with questions that are compelling, interesting, and are going to challenge that person. Find out what that person is all about and you will find that when you need help getting that next job, here is a person who will stand shoulder to shoulder with you.

This is the case because most people do not generally take initiative. Those who do and who combine that with a respect for people who have acquired success stand out. I'm talking about people who approach you and say "I want to ask you a bunch of questions and I'm just curious" and are not asking for anything in return. Those people will make a solid impression.

If I know of somebody within my network who is looking for

a new employee, and I have someone else who has sought me and offered to compensate me for my time, I am going to tell that person who is hiring, "You should check out this person who offered to pay me for an informational interview, which I thought was so unique and such a cool hook."

When I was first starting out, my father introduced me to Andy Russell, who at the time was the president of AGA, and said, "Just go on an informational interview." Because of that informational interview, Andy was the second person (after my dad) I called after being laid off of Mediaplex. Andy created a job for me at the agency. He said, "We have enough sales people but we're going to create another business development role for you and let's figure it out. You're going to be our new sales guy." I blew it out of the water for him for the next three years.

We had bonded during that informational interview talking about, of all things, rugby. He played rugby at Princeton and I had played at Loyola, where I had my nose broken playing against the Naval Academy. "Yeah, those guys are great athletes," he said, laughing. We bonded over that and it paid off down the road.

If you want to sell to somebody, the first lesson is to stop selling. Instead, offer that person some sort of value. Come with curiosity and sit back and listen. Figure out what their pain points are. What are the things that are keeping them up at night? What are the things that are concerning them about their organization? Then, figure out how you can add value or make life easier. Selling 101: ask lots of questions. Add value after you ask those questions. If you don't have immediate answers, say, "I don't know but I'm going to find out for you." If your company can't offer the solution, find that solution somewhere else.

If the chief marketing officer is hiring your social media agency but they need a website design, channel partners in the best web design firm you can possibly find so that when you talk to that chief marketing officer, you can say, "Listen, we can solve the social media. We don't do the websites but we've got three really great people who do and a PR person if you're interested." That's coming with ideas, adding value, and asking the right questions. That's how you sell to somebody.

What if you want to network? Every time you go on a networking event, ask tons of questions. Prepare really compelling questions in advance. Email questions ahead of time to people who are going to be at a networking event. Schedule to meet a person at the event. That way, you have alleviated the need for that person to write a long email response and you can simply discuss things in person. Now, instead of a first impression, you are starting off on the fifth impression. You are already fast friends and are off to the races.

If you want to work at Acme Company, buy the URL Acme-CompanyShouldHireMe.com. I dare you. When I wanted to get involved in social media, I purchased the URL Facebook-ShouldHireMe.com. I was featured in FORTUNE *Magazine* for creative ways to gain employment. When I went on my first interview at Buddy Media, I brought the article with me and got the job. They knew I was passionate about social media. If you're that good and you really want that job at that company and you lust to be an employee at that company, create a blog with that URL and start giving that company everything that you will give them over the course of the next year—if you are that good. If you are, you will be able to conceive of 15 things of value that you can give to that company.

If you are following these pillars and are coming up with ideas, defining your passion, approaching it with focus, meditating, monitoring your health, and surrounding yourself with positive people, you will have a slew of ideas. Go ahead and target that company and tweet your website to their CEO. Reach out to their executives on LinkedIn and send emails to them saying, "I am passionate about being an employee at your organization. I bought this URL. All I want to do is work for you." Do that and I can almost guarantee that you're going to get that job.

WHERE YOU WILL GO

"Success dwells at the fulcrum of passion and excellence."
— CHRIS DESSI, FOUNDER/CEO, SILVERBACK SOCIAL

SUCCESS IN BUSINESS IS BORN FROM THE BUILDING of strong personal relationships. Leveraging modern technology, as I have prescribed, is in no way a selfish, egocentric, or egomaniacal endeavor despite some lingering perceptions to the contrary. In fact, by following the guidelines that I've laid out above, you will be able to further build interpersonal relationships and give back to others in a way never before possible.

The playing field has been leveled by this technology. Now

everyone, regardless of their face to face comfort or skills, is able to network with a virtual persona that is just as gregarious and outgoing as someone like me. The necessities that are required are vulnerability, honesty, and authenticity. Your weaknesses in the real world need not hinder you in the digital one. Neither do the old rules apply.

Take, for example, someone who wants to be an actor. Previously, the job required you to move out to Los Angeles, become a waiter or waitress, and go out on auditions all day. If you are passionate about acting and have the chops for it, you can expedite the process and bypass the old methods by creating a YouTube channel and, instead of waiting for auditions to come to you, simply take the initiative and perform your own casting call for yourself. Maybe you choose favorite scenes from movies you like and offer your own performance. With a well-lit room and a decent camera, you've got a studio. Upload your audition to your channel and now you've bypassed the old gatekeepers.

A year or two goes by and you're not getting traction on your acting career. Instead of being stuck as a career server or two years behind on a different career path and trying to make rent in Los Angeles, you still have your regular 9-5 job and your same life. What have you lost? You tested the waters with your toe rather than by jumping in head first.

Tackling the pillars I've presented is similar to working the steps in a program. There are seven days' worth of pillars. Each day, you can be working on a different area of your personal brand. Always be learning because there is no definitive road map to success, although I've offered a template here that you can emulate. But the truth is, there are a variety of paths to success and today's pioneers blaze their own.

There is a joy in designing the life that you want to lead. The old days of punching a clock, acquiring tenure, and, one day, receiving a gold watch for your 30 years with the company are over, and you will be miserable if you are not flexible enough to adapt. To do that, you must continuously be challenging yourself, aggressively reading, listening to audiobooks or podcasts, or doing whatever is necessary in your line of work to stay ahead of the curve.

Victories, even very small victories, will keep you going. Your habits will create momentum, so instead of downward momentum, why not choose to move the ball down the field? You now have a plan of action. Follow the steps, become introspective, meditate on it, think about it, consult outside sources, read a book that inspires you.

James Altucher is an author who challenges me. He's written blog posts in which he says, "If you don't cringe right before you hit publish, then it ain't good." He explains that you have to allow yourself to open up a little bit, and I think that's really powerful. Once you start doing that, it's like training a muscle, and you become a little bit more comfortable, sharing a little bit more and taking more of a baby step, and you begin to create momentum which builds upon itself like compound interest. Once you get a little bit of positive feedback, you then resolve to get more positive feedback.

By generating interesting content, you are starting a dialogue in which people begin to follow your content and comments, and there is back-and-forth and a beautiful reciprocity ensues. And the next thing you know, you're firing on all cylinders, giving and receiving valuable information and experiences with others in a like-minded community.

That is why I wrote this book. This is me offering the knowledge that I've acquired in an easy-to-understand format for anyone who will but take the time to listen and choose to do the same in their own lives. My desire is that this will have a snowball effect as others begin to define their personal brands around the things that make them happy and healthy. That's the world I want to live in and those are the people I want to be around.

Hierarchies don't work. Paying your dues is a scam. Get those old-fashioned notions out of your head and take control of your own destiny. You have the knowledge and you have the tools. Following these pillars will bring your life fulfillment by creating more and stronger relationships, and that is the path to happiness and greatness. And if you're not here to do great things, vote yourself off the island right now.

I'm not saying that your content is going to land you on television, but I've seen it happen. I've lived it. I've seen people blog consistently about something that they're passionate about and they get a book deal because they generate really good content. And if that content is authentic, coming from your core, others will be drawn to it. And when others are drawn to it, they connect you with like-minded people, which might mean paid speaking gigs or it might mean paying you for ads on your blog, which, in turn might mean putting you in front of a TV camera. If you're an actor or a screenwriter, maybe it means a movie deal. If you're an athlete and you post your highlight reel, maybe it means a scholarship or a workout with a sports team.

The point is, no matter what it is that you're putting out there, the opportunities will come to you. Be proactive and you can, with laser-like precision, define your network the way you want. I guarantee you that if you start generating content from a genuine place and daily work those seven pillars, the most amazing, beautiful, exciting, thrilling opportunities will start to land in your lap.

You are remarkable. Once you embrace that, remarkable things will begin happening to you. It happens every day of the week to people around the world. Why not start today? Why not you?

ABOUT THE AUTHOR

AN AWARD WINNING DIGITAL THINKER, AUTHOR, TELE-vision & radio commentator, public speaker and educator, Chris Dessi is the CEO and Founder of Silverback Social. Silverback is an award winning digital marketing agency.

Throughout his career in London and New York, Chris has worked with a wide array of businesses ranging from start-ups to Fortune 500 companies, as well as notable personalities, products and brands. Chris travels the country coaching executives and college students how to leverage social media to benefit their personal brand message and their career. He regularly appears on CNBC, MSNBC, CNN, Fox News, Good Day New York, & FOX BUSINESS's Varney & Co. He's been quoted in Mashable, has lectured to the United States Marines aboard the Intrepid Sea Air & Space Museum, and was selected by the Business Council of Westchester's 40 Under 40 for exemplifying leadership. He is also a contributor to Inc.com and Success.com.

He has written three books, including this one: a leading social media book titled Your World is Exploding: How Social Media is Changing Everything—and How you Need to Change with it, and Just Like You: 24 Interviews of Ordinary People Who've Achieved Extraordinary Success, a motivational look into the lives of successful people in Chris's network.

Made in the USA
San Bernardino, CA
05 July 2016